prêt

à

-   -

porter

Robert Altman's

prêt-à-porter

Script by
Robert Altman,
Barbara Shulgasser,
and Brian D. Leitch
Introductions and
Interviews by
Brian D. Leitch
Art Direction by
Fabien Baron
Design by
Malin Ericson
Editorial Director
Francesca Gonshaw

BOXTREE

Contents

Prêt-à-Porter translated means ready-to-wear.

Ready-to-wear means mass-produced fashion. Fashion, as everybody knows, is all about clothes. This doesn't sound complicated until you add style. Without style, we would not need to reinvent fashion every six months. A great many people pay no attention whatsoever to style. The director Robert Altman was once one of them.

Arriving in Paris, where everyone, including the café waiter, has an opinion on what is chic, changed that for Altman. He went to a fashion show. He saw an awful lot of different scenes, on and off the runway. They were usually very dramatic, and they conveyed a sense of great struggle. Following the elliptical path of that struggle, one which started with an idea for a collection of clothes and ended with an "image," a product that was more than _that_ dress with _those_ shoes, more than the cut of the cloth, the smell of the perfume, the girl in the ad, or the name on the label. He saw another side of celebrity that he hadn't been attuned to in the past: the designer and the supermodel. Curious as they were, and contrary to all the brouhaha surrounding his nosing around their neck of the woods, he wasn't impressed. He wasn't unimpressed, either. Each one has "an act," as he says, and some are very good. Some are smart. Some are fun. Make no mistake about it, he says, some are real artists. But he never made a movie about them until now. The closest he ever came was a 1958 short about Kansas City couturier Nellie Donn.

The film _Prêt-à-Porter_ is more about the crispy, flaky outside than the soft, chewy, delicious center. It's about the people fashion designers associate with, who make the related product, who talk among themselves about it, and then spread the news. It's about the magazine editors and the media. "I don't really deal with the designers and what they do," Altman says. "My ragout is a farce, because I think farce is closer to reality than drama. Farcical things are happening all the time, mistakes are being made, and people enjoy that. People don't know how to behave in most situations, so they get an act, they rely on clichés, they make big, funny, embarrassing gaffes."

Because it's founded on the idea of sophistication, fashion abhors farce—it's too lowbrow. Prêt-à-Porter, the lowbrow farce, the view of an outsider, is not as chic and beautiful as fashion, at its very best, can be. Not even close. But it succeeds where the person who knows it all fails. It has the unglamorous glint of truth: a smudge here, a splotch there, like the pills on a cashmere cardigan or the dog shit on the bottom of a Manolo Blahnik shoe.

Altman likes to create an event and watch it happen. He'll take whatever path presents itself, because he trusts that every actor he casts will create a character that interests him. There are thirty-eight stars in Prêt-à-Porter. Some just play themselves, which, if you're Cher or Elsa Klensch, can be very interesting. "I can find better actors than any of you people," Altman said slyly just before directing a big scene, "but I need to see your famous faces, so people can follow this, so they'll go, 'Oh, it's you. It's Sophia Loren. I remember you.'" Altman loves the actors but tells them so little that they're forced to find their own way home. They collaborate in the storytelling, and if they didn't feel they had his wholehearted support, they'd run. Many do the best work they've ever done this way.

Perhaps what the director, the designers, and the stars have to say in this book will help to answer some of the questions languishing between the lines of the screenplay. Prêt-à-Porter is just one film in a large body of work. It's also the hardest thing, Altman says, he's ever done.

When he asked a couple dozen top models to strip down to nothing for Prêt-à-Porter's pivotal nude fashion show scene, the girl who was a Mormon did it, the girl with the large orange birthmark did it, and the one who was eight-and-a-half months pregnant did it with elegant self-containment. When the scene was finished, it was very quiet, and everyone was speechless. Robert Altman expects people to wait and see what they should say. Of course the media will eventually tell them. Honoré de Balzac, who could not attend, said, "He who sees only fashion in fashion is nothing but a fool."

   —Brian D. Leitch

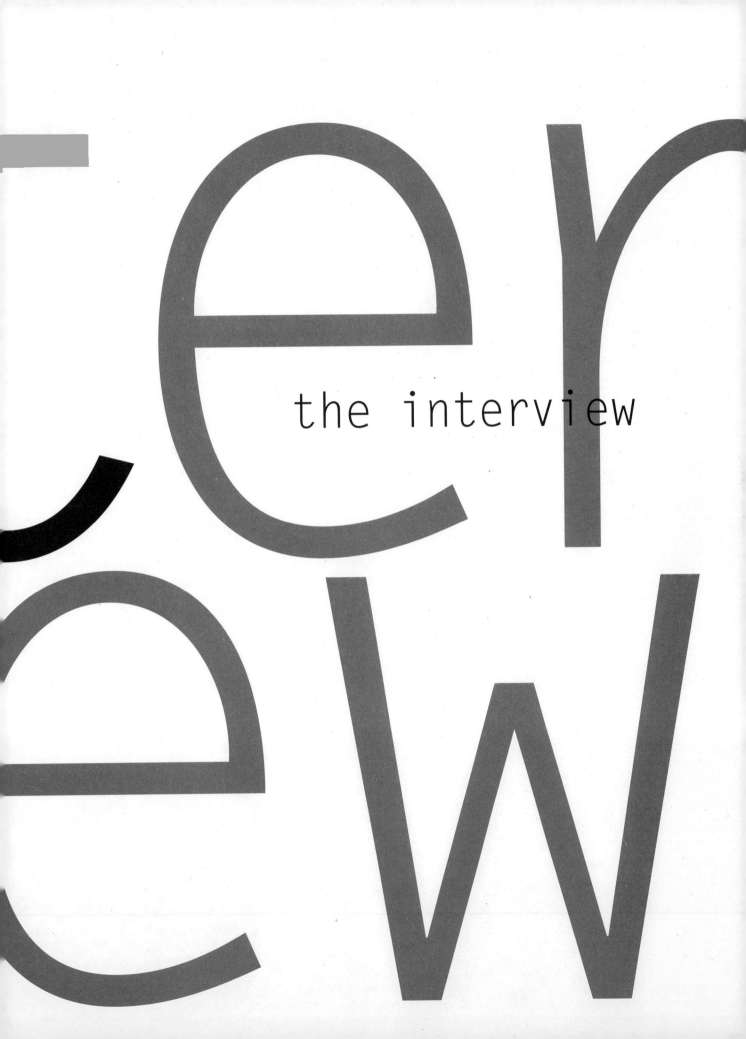

the interview

BrianD.
Leitch:
Prêt-à-Porter

has had a very long gestation, maybe three decades in the making. It seems you've been intrigued by this scene, and by the people in and around it, since the 1950s, when you made Fashion Fair, a 30-minute film, and later The Model's Handbook with Eileen Ford of Ford Models.

Robert Altman:

Yes, Suzy Parker was in on that, too. I forgot about those things. I guess that does go back through the years. It's been there, in some part of my subconscious mind, it's true.

L: What did you want to show about fashion with <u>The Model's Handbook</u> and <u>Fashion Fair</u>?

A: Well, the thing that would have attracted me to it at that time in my life was simply the glamour of it. I was trying to make films in Kansas City. Yes, I saw some glamour in it—but it was an excuse—I mean, girls in bathing suits but with the illusion of being dignified, highbrow. So I suppose that had something to do with it, me trying to elevate the level of what I was really doing, which if we strip it down, I suppose, is really "T and A."

L: It was about women.

A: Yes. The thing I did with Eileen Ford was actually an exercise video—aerobics—but you didn't call it that then. The other was this little short about Nellie Donn, who was the big designer of Kansas City—you know, $17 dresses! That was one of the first color pieces on CBS, I think. I'm not sure about all this. Then I did another one about Lilly Dache hats

L: Oh, Lilly Dache, sure.

A: I remember I shot it in the basement of some deserted building. I had sets sketched on big paper and models with hats. I forgot about that, so I guess there is something in my psyche about that stuff.

L: Fashion Fair was exactly what? It was a thirty-minute film. Was it meant to be a pilot?

A: Oh, I don't know. We had shots of a TWA hostess walking down the street, following her feet with the camera. I don't remember why we did those things, but you know, in the beginning, that era when I was trying to get started in film, like most people, you shot anything. You shot little short films; in fact, that's about all you could afford to shoot. I was working at that time for an industrial film company [Kelvin]. We did real nuts-and-bolts films, and the idea of doing anything that was away from this business kind of film thing was interesting—and then add the pretty girls.

L: So then about ten years go by, various scripts get written, and you move to Paris?

A: Prêt-à-Porter as we know it started in '84. I was in Paris showing Streamers with my wife, Kathryn, and I said, "What do you want to do?" And she said she'd love to see a fashion show, she'd never been to one. It happened to be during Prêt-à-Porter—I didn't even know what that meant—and so we went. I had no interest in going; in fact, I tried hard to get out of it. It was raining, and I had a dreadful hangover. I'd had very little sleep. The minute that show started, the music hit, I just thought, Wow! This is the circus! This is great! It even brought tears to my eyes. I thought, I've got to make a film about this. And I went backstage and talked to Sonia Rykiel, the designer. I started thinking about it. I felt so strongly about it that I literally moved to Paris and I did a couple of other things there, but I was trying to develop this picture.

L: Unsurprisingly, the Paris fashion world is, by turns, beautiful and grotesque. It seems that the country music world—or any world that has its myopic obsessives—is that way, too.

A: I think that many designers are hype artists but that the majority of these people are real artists. That's very clear. But it's like filmmakers. They're artists, but the people they associate with, who make the related product, they're hype. The Player was not about art, it was about hype. It's the same with Prêt-à-Porter. Actually, I don't really deal very much with the designers and what they do. It's

Meteo Roberto P.a.P
ROBERTO ALTMAN
Kim Basinger
BENEGAS

Robert Altman
P.a.P BENEGAS
KIM BASINGER

Robert Altman P.a.P.
A.F.   AUTOMNE HIVER
BENEGAS
P.M.
Kim. Basinger

ROBERT ALTMAN /P.A.P
BENEGAS
P.M.

P.a.P R. ALTMAN
BENEGAS
P.M.
Lorent BACALL

Robert Altman
P.a.P. BENEGAS
P.M.

BENEGAS
R. RIKIEL
S. Kim Basinger

ROBERT ALTMAN /P.A.P
BENEGAS
P.M.

ROBERT ALTMAN /P.A.P
BENEGAS
P.M.
Shophi LORENT-

ROBERT ALTMAN /P.A.P
BENEGAS
P.M.

P.M.
CERUTTI avec Robert
P.a.P ALTMAN
BENEGAS

ROBERT ALTMAN /P.A.P
BENEGAS
P.M.
MARCELO MASTROYANI
J. Rochefort

K.L.
RAOUL BENEGAS
SPRING / SUMMER 94
Roberto ALTMAN /P.a.P
Claudia Schifer

Robert ALTMAN
P.A.P.   AUTOMNE HIVER
BENEGAS
P.M.

CERUTTI
P.A.P Robert Altman
BENEGAS
P.M.

© IMAPRESS 4032902
PH: YANNIS VLAMOS OR
PRET A PORTER UN FILM
DE R. ALTMAN
Sophia LOREN

P.M.
BENEGAS
S. RIKIEL
Sophia Loren

P.M.
CERUTTI
P.a.P Robert Altman

Robert ALTMAN
P.a.P BENEGAS

BENEGAS
Sophia Lorent
CERUTTI
P.a.P R. ALTMAN
P.M.

more about media and related product and hype.

L: Well, one thing that you do is provide real footage of real fashion.

A: When we got ready to shoot this, I thought, "Shit, I don't really have any valid drama here! The only thing I can resort to is farce." In order to make that farce make sense, to make that farce become art, it has to be contradictory farce. When we did the first cut of this film, we had none of the real fashion shows. We put it together, we ran it, and it was three and a half hours long. And we looked at it, and I thought, Jesus, we're really in serious trouble! I thought, I just can't go and stick in those fucking fashion shows—they don't mean anything. But eventually we did it because we had to, we were obligated to, and suddenly I realized, oh, this is more important than all this stuff I made up!

L: Why?

A: Because it's real! And its reality validated the farce. When Kim Basinger showed up we had to start to work about the day that she got there. I mean, she had no time at all, and we started doing those things off of those cue cards, and she wasn't remembering that stuff. Everybody was kind of appalled, including me. Then I thought, "Oh fuck it, why not do it that way?" And it worked out well. Instead of composing the shot to expose that that's what she was doing, I let it happen. I let everything happen accidentally that we saw. I kept thinking, I'm not getting enough shots of Sophie [Chiara Mastroianni] holding the cards, so the audience realizes that's what she's doing. But by not getting those shots, I wasn't sitting there explaining to the audience what was happening or justifying what was happening— suddenly you catch on! You kind of get it, and then I realized Kim's smarter than I am about this thing, and when I redid that dueling-microphones scene with Elsa Klensch [CNN's style reporter] and Kim, just about nothing happened! And the reason nothing happened was that Elsa Klensch really has the same information to go on that Kim Basinger did: nothing! So you can write it for those short bites, which make it work on television, but it isn't like that on film. Not this film. You see it all. By catching her, by exposing her lack of knowledge or sophistication, by letting the audience see that, work for it, I think that makes Kim come out as strong as anybody in the movie—stronger, because certainly she becomes more believable than anybody else and because what she's doing is honest, she's showing the runs in her stocking, she's showing the...

L: Mistakes that she makes.

A: Yes, she's letting it hang out. That eventually became the kind of steel in the film. If the film works, and I think it's going to work, it comes from all those individual actors who were out there protecting themselves one way or another, taking chances. Stephen Rea too. First, I said, I can't get this actor down here. I haven't even got a part for him; this is no part. His work becomes one of the strongest things in it. All of these things developed. Danny Aiello's cross-dressing scene initially was an ignorant joke that didn't work at all, and now I think it works, because instead of trying to mock the character in this cross-dressing thing, and hype it in a kind of farcical manner, I went totally the other way. We just let him be caught in that situation—we didn't make fun of those people. We didn't get comedic about the cross-dressers, and my confidence in that comes from the fact that I didn't tell any of those people what they should do.

L: An important distinction to make is that those people are not actors. They are real cross-dressers.

A: That's right, and they just did what they do. I didn't try to make heroes or fools out of them, one way or another.

L: You said many times that this was the hardest thing you've ever done.

A: It was. I mean, I wanted out of it, I just didn't want to do this. I'm not sure I even want to be associated with it! But I had to do it, and then I thought, God, it's going to be out there and my ass is going to be exposed and it may be the last thing I'll ever do...

L: At what point did that change?

A: Well, it never changed.

L: It still hasn't changed?

A: I still have great reservations about this film, and I don't know how it's going to be. I believe that there is honesty in my position in this, that if somebody says, "This is the worst piece of shit I've ever seen in my life, and goddamn he didn't have any idea what he was doing," I'd have to say, "You're right." And if somebody came along and said, "This is the greatest fucking filmmaking," I'm going to say, "Great!"

L: How do you feel about it right now?

A: I think when I start seeing which side people start lining up on— then I'll tell you. One thing is sure: If people line up against the film, then I'll probably come out fighting.

L: Is "people" the audience or the critics?

A: Everybody. It's the whole.

L: You once said that as far as you're concerned, the audience is responsible for a lousy movie, because the audience likes lousy movies and puts its money down to go and see lousy movies.

A: That's right.

L: On the one hand, you want people to like it, and then on the other hand, you don't have much faith in what people like.

A: But a lot of that kind of talk is armor, a defense mechanism to protect myself when the flak starts flying. And if it starts flying in my direction and everybody's against it, I'll take a position of valor. I'll defend it in whatever way I can.

17

L: In artistic terms.

A: Yes. In artistic terms, I'll never disown it. I'll never try to distance myself from it. It's a puzzle. But then I don't know what else there is to do. If you go and say, I'm following a pattern that I know I'm safe with, that isn't very courageous.

L: So what makes the stakes so high with Prêt-à-Porter?

A: Maybe the amount of time I've put in, maybe the hoopla that's gone along with it, maybe the anticipation that seems to be so high. The publicity level is staggering. I felt very solid with Short Cuts. With The Player, I felt pretty much the same way as this. I would have bailed out of The Player even after the first cut of the film. And all the time I never thought we were doing anything. I was experimenting, but I never had any great confidence with The Player. I feel kind of the same way about this. I don't know, it's just a strange thing. After I show this to sixty people next week, I'll have totally different ideas, I expect. I've got to see if what remains will lift this above farce—if it's received by the audience at the proper level.

L: From what I can tell, the comedy in this film is on all different levels. There is farce, there are sophisticated inside jokes, there is allegorical humor, there's the goofy whodunit.

A: That was also true of Nashville. There's cross-cultural, multi-lingual humor too. Shuffling the number of cards that I have to make this deck, it's going to be very interesting.

L: At one point you said you wouldn't have made this movie if you couldn't have Marcello Mastroianni, if he couldn't do it.

A: I don't know if that's true or not. It could have been true. He was one of my key players. Sophia has become as important to this as Marcello. For a long time I didn't know if I could use Sophia, to the point that I almost alienated her. I didn't contact her until the end of November, and she was getting pretty pissed off by then, but I didn't know if I could use the Italian idea—I was thinking of using a French person.

L: There are four or five languages in the film, if you count Russian, Italian, French, English, Spanish, so there's a lot of miscommunication, a lot of room to be misunderstood.

A: That was always part of the knit. This is probably going to be the first film that's truly international—in which anyone's attempted all of this. This film is going to look pretty shitty when it gets dubbed in German!

L: I bring up the whole idea of miscommunication because you've said before that the film is as much or more about the press and about the various fashion acolytes sort of hanging around talking as it is about the designers.

A: Oh, absolutely.

l'arrivée de Marcello

L: Teri Garr, who plays Major's wife, goes shopping in Paris and has no idea what anyone's saying around her, but she tries. And you have Tracey Ullman, Linda Hunt, and Sally Kellerman playing three magazine editors who are also largely ignorant of everything going on around them, and that's all based on language. It's their business to come to Paris, this very beautiful and very foreign place and try to communicate something about fashion, to bring it back home to America and tell you what it is, what it means...

A: And they bring it back not only with confidence but with arrogance!

L: Let's talk about the nude fashion show, which comes at the end of the movie.

A: These are girls who are not porno stars. These are not girls who go out and walk around naked and publicly expose themselves. These are all real honest-to-god runway models, and the very fact that they did that, the way that they did that, I think it's going to be sidestepped. I mean, it's going to be commented on, but nobody's going to know what to say. They'll be afraid—nobody will want to make the first call on it. So it's generally going to go uncalled. In other words, my feeling is that these girls aren't going to be chastised for it, except by their grandmothers. It's just going to sit there.

L: Is this scene the most important of the film?

A: Oh, obviously. If that scene wasn't in the film, this film would have nothing. In other words, that scene, and Kitty Potter's speech at the end of it, are what will make this film valid. Because there were no editorial comments about what happened; it just happened. And Kitty Potter gives her audience a sound bite, as Kitty Potter would, and then suddenly she says, "What the fuck am I talking about? Is everybody crazy? Did I just see a bunch of naked women out there on that stage? What the hell is that? Blah, blah, blah, I'm out of here." And that is going to vindicate the whole film.

L: Now I need to backtrack and ask you to tell me what the nude fashion show is about.

A: Well, it's The Emperor's New Clothes, I guess. It's that and much more. It's what fashion's about. And Kitty says it all. But that kind of thing taking place says something about what the whole flap is about. The show went on, the money was spent, the audience was there, music played, and there were no clothes.

L: But there was wild applause at the end. They got what they came for.

A: Oh, yes.

L: The audience, who were all Paris fashion types, didn't know what they were going to see—they filed in and they sat down. They weren't expecting a nude show.

A: Even the ones that did know, didn't quite believe that was what they were going to see, and then when they saw it, they stood up and they applauded. Of course, I think that the saving grace of that show was the pregnant bride at the end [Ute Lemper], because that took the sex out of it—that took the titillation out of it. Yet it's something they want to see and are kind of fascinated to see, but they don't know why they are responding to it. This is what I anticipate. Now, the critics, they would say that wasn't truthful. Those girls were all shaved, that's unnatural. Or they're going to say, they were all beautiful girls, or whatever they say, I don't much care.

L: But if you deal with this at the plot level, those girls did it for this character called Simone Lo. She asked them for help, for solidarity, and every single one of them came through for her.

A: Yes, because they understood it. And every one of those girls did it for me, too—they understood the picture on a certain level also. So it wasn't for exhibitionists. They certainly didn't do it for the money, or they didn't do it because they thought it was going to help their career. I think, in fact, most of them sat back and said, "Jeez, maybe I shouldn't have done this." Ute puts herself in this position, when a woman does not want to show herself naked.

L: Right, the least sexual moment, eight-and-a-half months pregnant.

A: That's right, and I mean, she's literally unfuckable.

L: Just logistically!

A: The thing about it—the reason I'm nervous about it—is that this is new ground. This is new territory for this art, not greatly new, but slightly new. There isn't anything out there like this that anybody's seen before. It's not about what the fashion world is going to make of it. I don't have any idea. The country-and-western world hated <u>Nashville</u>. They stayed away, they publicly disowned it. They said, "That's not good music!" But I didn't try to achieve good or bad music. I said, "Oh, okay, let's use that song, it's great; or that song, it's really awful, isn't it?"

L: It runs the gamut.

A: Yes, and that's what we're trying to do here.

L: The fashion in this film also runs the gamut—from ripped-up, inside-out clothes to Avenue Montaigne elegance.

A: Sonia Rykiel was appalled with Xüly Bet!

L: On a documentary level, it's a moment in time, the state of the art, 1994.

A: This year, right now.

L: In a sense, you've made a movie about how the media depicts the world of style and fashion.

A: Have I? I mean, I don't know what this movie is really about. I think I'll find out in time. People will tell me what it's about, and then I'll agree and I'll say, "Oh, yes, that's what I had in mind." Some of it's calculated, but most of it's done intuitively or instinctively. It's just something that occurs to me. I don't know what my real reasons are.

L: What about the style of the film? You're an auteur—speak!

A: I keep the camera moving pretty much, and a lot of people, they're more used to it now. But back in the 70s, when I started doing that, people got very irritated. They said, "You zoom-lens too much." I was trying to do it with the zoom or moving around a lot, and they said, "That's not the way to make pictures."

L: Because it was jittery—too much continuous movement all the time?

A: Yes, and it was new then. Now it's more common, and the old method of shooting is more <u>Masterpiece Theatre</u>. What we're trying to do now is hide more than we're trying to show, because the audience sees so much—they see everything—and I'm trying to make them bend their necks a little bit. I like to have a sort of obstruction in front of things so the audience feels they're at the back of a crowd, and they want to be in on what's going on there. "Did I miss something?" they'll wonder. Sitting there in their seats, they should feel that they have to be alert.

L: You once said that your creative work is 90 percent done with the casting.

A: Well, the actors take over. I think that the first person I cast in this picture was Lauren Bacall.

L: You cast her ten years ago?

A: I met her at some premiere at Tavern on the Green (in New York), you know, and I said, "I'm going to do this fashion film, and I want you to be in it. I want you to play Diana Vreeland."

L: Which she doesn't, but anyway...

A: Yes. And so she was the first one on the picture. And who came in after that?

L: A lot of these people you've worked with before: Sally, certainly, and Julia, Tim, Lyle, Linda—you've worked with all of them on <u>Short Cuts</u>, <u>Popeye</u>, <u>M*A*S*H</u>, and so on. Stephen Rea, whom you've never worked with before, told me that he felt like he had spent six months auditioning for you, because he was sort of slowly getting to know you—coming to dinner and hanging out with you—and that it was like six months of foreplay.

A: That's not quite true. Over a period of time I got to know Stephen Rea, and he's somebody I liked very much. I just never could think of a role, I mean he's not easily castable in a film, in a new American film.

L: Because he's Irish.

A: Yes, and so when this thing came up I said, "Oh, I want to put you in this thing! The photographer! I'll make him Irish," because I was trying to make this multinational, polyglot. I worried about him after he said yes for a long time, because in the development of the script this character didn't have any place to go really. He was just kind of there. I get myself in this spot quite often. I'll get

somebody, I'll say, "Oh, he can play so and so," and then I find out
that there is no so and so.

L: So how do you get out of that?

A: I have to keep working! He became a key character, but it was down
to the wire when that happened. Meanwhile, they wanted him very much
for that Roman Polanski film, and I kept saying, you should take
that! He said, "No, I want to do your film," and I thought, "Oh,
Christ, I'm going to keep him out of that film, and then I'm going to
have nothing for him to do in this film." As it turned out, he's one
of the real strong focal points in the film.

L: The film makes no bones about saying that in the fashion world, the
photographer is God. He was God. Everybody's vying for his attention.

A: He worked on it, he figured that out, and he's very, very smart, a
very gifted actor. He's got this sudden stardom. Yesterday nobody
knew who the fuck he was.

L: Before <u>The Crying Game</u>.

A: He's been acting and acting. He's a very, very strong journeyman
actor, and now suddenly he's wanted for all these roles because the
public recognizes him. It teaches you or me that anybody can play any
part, almost. You don't have to keep putting actors in things they've
done before.

L: There's no more encouraging evidence of that than what the Kitty
Potter character went through. You plowed through half a dozen
actresses.

A: I went from Lily Tomlin to Anjelica Huston to Meryl Streep...

L: Back to Lily Tomlin.

A: Back to Lily Tomlin and even to Lili Taylor for a minute, and then
even to abandoning the thing, and then at the last minute Kim
Basinger.

L: You worked with her before too, on <u>Fool for Love</u>.

A: Oh, yes.

L: So Kitty went from being a cool, chic Huston type to a wry, witty
Tomlin type to a mannered Streep type, to finally, a kind of Southern
belle idiot who turns out to be no idiot at all.

A: The character would have been how any of those women would have
played it, and ultimately it didn't make any difference to me. I
mean, nothing depended upon how that part was played. If Meryl Streep
had done it I'd probably be sitting here saying, "Oh Jesus! What a
break. Thank God we got Meryl Streep!" Same for the rest. Now I can't
imagine this picture without Kim being Kitty—but this always happens,
because actually the part is created by the actor who plays it. In
other words, it's just a blank space when I'm thinking about it.

L: Just before you were about to shoot at the airport, and you had a
big group of actors—they were all arriving in Paris in this scene—you
made an announcement: You said to them, "Listen, all you people, I

can find much better actors than any of you to be in this film, but I want to see your faces, because you're famous faces, and we'll be able to follow you through this movie because of your faces. So I want to see you! All of you!" Everybody kind of laughed and got nervous at the same time, and then they did their stuff.

A: There is truth in that. What I was saying to them was these parts could be played by anybody, but the reason I needed recognizable faces is because there are so many characters. There is no plot, so the audience sees Kim Basinger or Sophia Loren, they know who that is. When they see them the next time, they don't have to stop and wonder who's that. Some of these films with a lot of characters are cast with people who are unknown generally, and they may be brilliant actors, but when there are too many of them you get mixed up. Was that his wife or his girlfriend? The idea of using icons in these parts immediately brings information to the audience.

L: Now around the time that you were making M*A*S*H, Ingo Preminger said, "Robert Altman has a weakness: He loves unattractive people." In fact, you were originally against the idea of Sally Kellerman for Hot Lips, because she was too beautiful. And now of course you're working with people like Julia Roberts and Kim Basinger, and the subject is so-called beautiful people—fashionable people, models. So I'm just wondering how you feel about that.

A: He's right and he's wrong, because what he's talking about is the attitude of the industry itself, the commercial film industry, and that is simply to fill the screen with beautiful people. I find that most people aren't beautiful, until they open their mouth and you get to know them a little bit. I was using Shelley Duvall, and people screamed, "Oh, God, you've got to get somebody else." I can't tell you the number of producers who've said to me, "Listen, get somebody up there I want to fuck." That's what it's all about, and I just find that abhorrent. That isn't what it's all about, and if it is what it's all about, I don't want to be all about it with them, because it doesn't interest me.

L: But with this film you're dealing essentially with the world of beautiful people. You look at what's coming down the runway, and these girls are extraordinary. You're making a film where you're surrounded by beautiful people.

A: They're not necessarily beautiful to me. I don't get off on Miss—whatever her name is—Linda Evangelista. I don't go, "Oh my God!" I mean, I see these guys around me that are kind of, hey, I'd like to screw her, but I don't really believe that they mean that.

L: It's expected of them.

A: Right. It's expected of them: Look at those tits! They start talking about big tits. I don't think big tits are particularly attractive or interesting and certainly aren't necessarily sexy.

Still, at my age I can sit with somebody and say, "Wow look at that babe!" And there's some really ugly girl walking down the street and her shorts are too short and her tits are kind of pushed up and out. I mean, she can be a kind of dragon, but she represents sex and so the guy that I'm talking to is saying that to me, but I don't think that he believes it, either. I just don't get it. When I was a kid that was never the way I looked very much. It never really interested me, and I never quite believed that it did anyone else. But, boy, they sure do go on about it.

L: Catherine Leterrier, the costume designer, told me that when you cast Sophia, you said you wanted her to be like the Eternal Woman, yes?

A: I don't know what the Eternal Woman is, but I wanted her to be what she represents. The mystique that surrounds Sophia Loren brought something to the film. She gave it a reason, another reason. She's not just a good actress playing that part. She's Sophia Loren, so she represents herself, and she represents all the movies that she was ever in, for instance, the strip scene with Sophia and Marcello.

L: It's an homage to an old film that they did together years and years ago.

A: It's from Yesterday, Today and Tomorrow, and we play the same music, the lingerie she wears is very much the same, Marcello is sitting on the bed...

L: And Marcello howled like a dog in that one, too.

A: Yes. If you don't know anything about that movie and you see this movie, this thing is still going to be as funny. But if you know or remember or even if you subliminally remember, it just gives you that much more. It's like tapestry—it gives you more depth, so what you're seeing is history. You're seeing the cartoon that I'm showing you today, but there's more.

L: While Sophia is giving this performance, she's drawing on this experience she had however many years ago. While she's stripping, the dialogue between them, which is ostensibly ad-libbed, is actually from the old movie.

A: Yes, she's doing it the same way, and at the same time, she gets the joke.

L: Tell me about "the three witches"—Sally Kellerman, Linda Hunt, and Tracey Ullman, who play the three Powers That Be in the world of fashion magazines.

A: I call them the three witches because there were three of them, and somehow that term stuck, and we put it into the script.

L: How did you decide to cast Linda Hunt? You launched her career with Popeye, didn't you?

A: Yes, and I think she's a terrific actress, and I just thought she would be a force.

L: She chooses her moments well in the film—she holds back where a

Tournge dans la tempête sur le Pont Alexandre III

lot of the other people hold forth, and it's interesting because she's so small.

A: Physically. Her size is part of what she's doing, so she doesn't have to project. It's her presence. If another character, a Miss Average Person, was in there, and held back, you'd never see her, sort of like Lyle [Lovett] in a way. I mean Lyle does nothing in this picture, and I'm afraid he might be criticized for it.

L: Why?

A: Because he doesn't really have anything to do, and he doesn't do anything extreme. He's just kind of there, being the rich guy from Texas. But that's exactly what I think that kind of character ought to be. I think of all those movies like Flying Down to Rio, all those Fred Astaire pictures. There was always the rich guy's son or the rich nebbish who was just there, and that's kind of what Lyle represented in this. Putting any personality into it would have been wrong.

L: It's curious, too, because Clint, the character, is such a benign personality, and yet he sets the whole chain of events in motion.

A: Yes, he's the guy who causes it, because he's the one who's got the money.

L: Lauren Bacall toppling on Anouk Aimee toppling on Rupert Everett and so on.

A: All of these smart people, and the guy with the money comes along and that's it.

L: So what about Lili Taylor, the feminist, lesbian reporter for the New York Times, who is secretly interested in clothes?

A: She's not particularly interested in clothes. She's interested in proving that she's not interested in clothes, and it takes as much work to not be interested as it does to be interested. So that's just a journalistic kind of character that I think exists. The lesbian thing will be almost impossible to discern, because it's hardly done, but it gave her something to play around with. It's just a couple of reference points. It's also not by way of criticism, and it's not by way of chastising, and it's not by way of making fun. This had to be represented.

L: When I was on the set watching you work with this huge polyglot of personalities—all big stars—it seemed as if what you were doing was withholding information from them.

A: They have to dig into their own resources to cover themselves and project themselves. And the more I tell them, the more excuse they have to say, "Well, that's what you wanted me to do and it's not my fault if you think it's no good."

L: So they have full responsibility for what they create?

A: We're in a big gray area here. The more responsibility they have, the more instinctively they will protect themselves, and hopefully, the better they will be. Then, at the same time, I have to give them the sense that I am not going to let them make assholes or fools of themselves.

L: Now that this picture is over, the shooting part of this picture is over, how do you feel about the improvisations that you got?

A: They're like all improvisations. Most of them are weak, but some great things came out of them. There's some very good stuff. I think it will work.

L: Did every actor create a character that you were interested in?

A: More or less. I'm not looking for extreme. I don't want that.

L: Just observing things on the set, it occurred to me that some people seemed to be playing the character and some people seemed just to be playing themselves.

A: Well, that's true.

L: And everyone—except Julia, who was in a tacky sweat suit with a nasty red wine stain on it, no makeup—was worried about how they looked. This, in a Robert Altman movie?

A: Most of them are really worried about how they look. There are mixed emotions there. They say, "Oh, I want to be The Actor." They love it when they can go and put dirt on their face, or they can emaciate themselves to play some extreme character. But when they get dressed up and then turn and bend over and the skirt splits and you see their underwear's dirty, they don't like that.

L: Why, because this is about prêt-à-porter?

A: Because it's too close to home. The audience won't know that I'm doing this on purpose. And, of course, we want the audience to think that all this is actually happening at the time, because the audience is who we're trying to seduce and to fool.

L: When you were shooting at the real shows, and you have these improvisational things going—little dialogues between actors mixed in with the real people—on film it tends to make the real people look like they're doing impersonations of themselves.

A: That's what they are.

L: And that's where the documentary element layered on top of the film element starts to mesh—the way you were talking about how important the real shows are to the film.

A: Yes, because the real people are acting every day. Ferré, Gaultier, Margiela—they're performing every time they're out in public doing their stuff. They're doing the same thing these actors are doing. It just happens to be <u>their</u> act.

L: At the Bulgari party, Kitty Potter [Kim Basinger] interviews Cher, and nobody was prepared for it. A dumbfounded Kim asks Cher what she thought about all this, and Cher responded, thinking that she meant the world of fashion, by saying, "Well, prêt-à-porter is"—I'm paraphrasing—"about sadness and loneliness, because none of us is ever going to be Christy Turlington or Naomi Campbell, and it's sad."

And Kim shot back with "None of us is ever going to be Cher, either," to which Cher replied, "I am a victim and a perpetrator." None of that was planned or scripted.

A: Cher's done hours and hours of that television stuff selling cosmetics and some products in commercials, so Cher's acting when she's doing that. So that's her act. But everybody has an act. I have an act, you have an act. You fall back on whatever gets you into safe, comfortable territory. That's why people can be hypnotized on stage. They're put in a position of extreme embarrassment, and the one thing they want to do is not be there, so they go out. They don't want to be where they are, and the hypnotist always keeps them at a point of embarrassment. The guy's saying, "Go to sleep," and you go to sleep because you prefer that. Those things are very real. Actors and people on camera end up doing the same thing. They go to the comfort zone. So I tell actors as little as possible, because if I tell them something, then they'll try to do it.

L: It won't be a performance, it won't please you.

A: It won't please me because it won't be usable. It won't be any good. So I'll sit and say: "Are you going to wear yellow? That's good, the yellow socks are good. I like the yellow socks." So you walk away. You've had some sense of approval, but it has nothing to do with your real question. So then when you are suddenly there to perform, you have nothing to fall back on. You do not have my words to fall back on. You can't say, "Well, this is what he told me to do, and if I'm no good that's his fault." So I avoid saying anything that they can really use. But I never want to make someone so uncomfortable that he or she wants to go into a state of hypnosis.

L: Every single one of these actors has responded to that by saying they have a deep, deep trust in what you're doing.

A: The general consensus is supposed to be that I know what I'm doing. I'm considered skillful. They say, "Oh, well, he knows." If none of them had ever heard of me before, none of them would be in the fucking movie. They want that security so they can say, "Even if this doesn't seem good to me, he's such a great director that he wouldn't do this unless it was right."

L: Little do they know!

A: Yes, but the truth is they'll get it right, because what I'm looking for is something I've never seen before.

L: What? Something you've never seen before?

A: If I've seen it before, or it's something I know, if I try to get you to imitate something, you'll fail because you won't imitate to what my scale is. I want you to show me something I believe. Some of the things we shot made me think, "Oh, so and so was terrible. They did nothing in this scene." Then I'd look at it editing and think, "That's great."

L: That seems to happen quite a lot.

A: That's why this is such a nervous time for me, the editing, putting the stuff together. I look at these scenes now with Anouk, and Anouk's terrific in this picture. She's different from all the other actors, and I kept her that way. You believe that she's got a depth that the rest of them don't have.

L: Fellini told you that dailies are the best movie, the real movie.

A: Yes, because that's everything that you could possibly have.

L: All the best stuff and all the worst stuff is there.

A: All the stuff. That's the universe you have to work.

L: Why do you like the actors and the crew and everybody to come sit in a theater and see the dailies every single day during the shoot?

A: Because you know they're working ten, twelve hours a day, very hard work, and it's sort of like you get a little sit-down to say, "Look what I did." It's sort of a reward for them, for their efforts. I know there are lots of people who shoot film who don't let anyone look at the dailies—it's real somber and serious. I know that there's a lot of that behind-closed-doors, nit-picking stuff that goes on, but not with my films.

L: They don't let anybody in on the process?

A: It's a criticism process looking at the dailies: "Look! That fucking scene is out of focus! Blah, blah, blah." It's just more pain, and I just think the actors and the crew who do all this work, and also take a lot of abuse because it's a whip-cracking cattle drive, should see it all now. By the time the film is released, and they can see it, they have probably shot two or three other films, and it's deep in their past. In a way, it's almost foreign to them. And the other thing I find is if I can encourage actors to show up, the crew members will show up. They learn from it, and the actors who show up will learn from the crew and also they'll learn to get themselves out of being so subjective. And when they start coming and rooting for someone else, suddenly their fellow actors become not competitors but collaborators. It's terrific. But I think there are many occasions when these people are competing against each other.

L: Did you think that on this set, with three dozen of the world's biggest stars all together waiting around for six or seven hours at a time to shoot, they would get competitive?

A: It put them in a position of almost policing themselves. There were so many of them that if one person started to act badly they had to suffer the glances and slings and arrows of their fellow workers. It puts them in a certain behavioral control group.

L: What I noticed on the set, the way it worked, was that eventually a subtle hierarchy started to emerge: There were splinter groups, lone wolves—wolvettes?—and there was a bully and a person that got picked on, and there were two mother figures, a kvetchy type and a

Madonna for everybody. I mean, without getting into who was what...

A: Absolutely. That's always the case. That comes out in any group whether you're in a day room in a sanitarium or whether you're on a baseball team. A society develops.

L: Is creating that society—you do work with a contingent of people that you know well, some for decades—is creating that society an important part of how the film is then created?

A: How the society is managed is important. You don't create the society, but how it's managed and how it works within itself becomes very important.

L: How did you manage this society?

A: I don't manage it. I let it manage itself. If something starts getting out of hand, starts trouble, I try to eliminate that source of trouble, try to alleviate it, try to put it in the most positive, pleasant kind of relief state so that everybody can have a good time, because everybody does work very hard. What you have to remember is that these actors are much different from the rest of us—they're up there, their ass is up there, they're exposed. And once that's on film, I mean, I'm gone. Nobody sees my face but they're up there every fucking time the thing's shown. If it's bad, it's bad every time. It never gets good. So they're nervous and rightly so, because they don't have any control. I can be up there and say that's great, do that again, and have them just make asses out of themselves and put it in the film. I can destroy them in some way, and that happens, I think. So my job is to try to give them the confidence they need in me, to trust that I will protect them, so that way they can feel free to take bigger chances. There's my job description.

L: There was a theory on the set among a few actors that when those kinds of eruptions took place in the society—bristling egos and problems and jealousies and infighting—that you in fact created that, that you allowed it, that you wanted to create a situation where there was this kind of thing going on.

A: No, that's not true. I'm aware that those kinds of things do happen and that the results of those kinds of things do affect performances and not necessarily badly. But I try very, very hard not to be manipulative in that manner, because if I get caught once, I'm finished. Once I've lost the trust of that person, once I've put him in a situation where he behaves badly, and I've allowed it, or encouraged it, he won't trust me again. Then I have nothing.

L: Obviously, all these actors, they all have a history with you, they all trust you and each them said at one point or other, "We're not doing it for the money, we're doing it because it's Bob."

A: The reason they want to work with Bob is because Bob lets them, encourages them, to do the work that they became actors to do in the first place. So many places it's "No, stay on that mark and look this way and say this and say it this way and say it this way and say that," and it's really no fun at all. They become puppets, totally controlled by somebody else. Here they also have each other—there's friction and jealousy and all kinds of emotion. Those things do reflect on the performance, and I allow them to reflect on the performance and many times they help the performance, because what we're really dealing with is human behavior: truthful behavior.

L: Everybody's always saying that film is the great twentieth-century art form.

A: Well, it's a medium.

L: But it has a life of its own. It reaches everyone, and there's so much possibility in film.

A: It's the most accessible. It travels. To do live theater, you can't have more than 500, 600 people at a time. Maybe with a musical, occasionally, you can go to 2,000. One minute of film can reach into billions of hours of viewing. After you're dead, people are still discovering you, even if you were dead before they were ever born. Christian Slater's behavior on film now, even after he's 90 years old and dead and buried, will remain. Kids will be born, and they'll see him, and they will also see a pretty accurate rendition of what kind of a person he was. Probably they'll view him as very contemporary somehow, so his exposure will only increase. But as filmmaking style changes, it will become period; in other words, there will come a time when that kind of acting and that kind of editing and staging and preparation won't be used. But it won't die.

L: There will be a different way of absorbing characters and truths and other kinds of information from film.

A: I think now it's up to a point where it's almost a one-to-one mirror image of human behavior. If human behavior changes, it will change with it.

L: You speak about art often, and you have a deep respect for art and artists. I think of you as one of the very, very few who could be called an auteur, who does it all, who creates from inception to completion. And then I think of Prêt-à-Porter as a film that fits into your monolith—this body of work.

A: Oh yes, it's a chapter.

L: When you made The Player, the critics said it was about the death of American filmmaking.

A: The death of American filmmaking took place long before that. It's hype.

L: Speaking of hype, the designer Nino Cerruti made an interesting analogy. He said: "Fashion is exactly like drugs. There are the people who make it, the people who sell it, and the people who use it." A drug, of course, is an illicit thing. The other thing about a drug is it provides a high or a buzz. I wonder what you think of that analogy.

A: I think it's good. Because I think, when I put nice clothes on, I think, "Oh God, I really look good. This is a terrific ensemble that I've achieved today." Other people might think I look okay, but I don't pay much attention to them. They don't pay much attention to me. So it really is a very personal thing. It's your trip. It doesn't transmit very far out of your own aura; if it did it would be dreadful.

L: Why?

A: Because then you are what you wear. It's something we fool ourselves with—we think, "Oh God, I look really good in this." I'll say, "Oh God, you look great today," if I know you've got something new on. I don't necessarily think it looks great. Maybe when I think about it, it's nice, but I'm saying it to make you feel good, because I know that when somebody says that to me it makes me feel good. A little social backrub.

L: It's a little dance everybody does.

A: Nobody really pays too much attention to what other people look like as long as they don't look so far out or dirty or stupid that it forces attention. I dressed differently during the making of this picture than I ever did before. I still have that wardrobe, but I find that I'm not wearing the ties today.

L: So you're on the other side of it.

A: I just kind of tired of it, but on the other hand, I think I will never be the way I was before.

L: Which was?

A: Which was almost thumbing my nose at it.

L: It's very chic to have a goatee like yours now.

A: I've seen a lot people wearing goatees now. I got tired of it once way back, and I remember shaving and seeing a double chin. I stopped immediately. That's been my main motivation to keep it. You do identify yourself with what you see in the mirror, and you say, "That's me, and that's what I represent."

L: You said during filming that this was the toughest thing you'd ever done.

A: It was.

L: Why?

A: Control. It was so spread out and freewheeling and rolling and... French. I don't speak the language, so it just takes longer, and it knocks a lot of the intuition and gossip out. So much of what people were saying and doing was totally gone.

L: But you plan to use that in a way, because you're going to use a lot of subtitling with different languages in the film.

A: Oh, absolutely. And I knew that that was going to happen. I was not expressing despair, I was expressing discomfort. I knew that was going to be one of the strongest points in the film.

L: It's almost like instead of overlapping dialogue and all of those things that you've used before, there is this babel of foreign languages.

A: In a way, it's easier because you don't hear the words. You can't understand it all, so you see the behavior and you kind of get it.

L: Tell me about TV, the use of television in your films.

A: It's another way of communication, but it's also part of the fabric of fashion, so why not use it? Also it helped me with the language—to continue reminding everybody that this thing is all shot in English, the dialogue is in English, and it's as much about France. So at least that keeps that alive in one form or another, as does somebody trying to speak French and doing it badly.

L: Which Teri Garr does to perfection.

A: And Betty Bacall. Television is part of American culture, part of French culture. Now its part of Albanian culture. It's here. It's everywhere. I don't think you can ever take it out of us, whether you like it or not.

L: How old are you now?

A: Sixty-nine.

L: Do you remember reading, a couple of years ago in The New Yorker, when Terrence Rafferty wrote: "At 67, Robert Altman is the youngest filmmaker in America"?

A: Terrence Rafferty wrote that? He didn't like Short Cuts at all. Well, I know what he's talking about. I like what it says.

L: What does it say?

A: That I haven't stopped, that's all. Most people quit at this stage. They get enough. You start to see this light at the end of the tunnel. In ten years I'm going to be dead. That affects everything that you do—the tendency is to slow down and close off. I'm trying to open something up out there, something that I don't know anything about, and let me fail, but it's fun. I don't want to stop now. I'd be bored to death. I'd rather be in prison where I'd be trying to figure out how to get out. I'm thinking about these two new films that I've still got to do, and I've got to be really careful—careful not to ever let myself think I know how to do this. I want to do something I don't know how to do.

L: You did that on Prêt-à-Porter, didn't you?

A: Probably, but I've no obligation other than to preserve my own joy for me. Thirty years ago they said, "You're going to get $12 million a year to the end of your life. You've got this television series you own [M*A*S*H], blah, blah, blah," and if I'd listened I'd be dead a long time by now. We wouldn't be having this conversation. So I just try to keep going, but it's not for any reason other than that I know it's fun, it's exciting, it's how I have a good time. That's all it's about. I mean the failures and the successes, the way you're perceived in the world, don't really make any difference, because when you really get right down to the crunch, it's my own selfish ego that I'm dealing with.

L: And whether or not you're having a good time.

A: Absolutely. And a good time means the pain of accomplishing something. I know I could get slapped right across the face. It happens, I know that. But the slap in the face means you can start again. If you don't get the slap in the face, I don't know what it means. You probably die. It's trying to create, each time, a little something beyond what you see as possible. It's like being a pilot today is probably not very much fun—you've got union rules and regulations. But being a pilot fifty years ago or seventy years ago was a lot of fun.

L: There was a lot of crashing into cliffsides seventy years ago. That must have been painful.

A: Yes. It's part of the thing you're doing, part of the project, and until you find it, you haven't pushed out far enough. Look at an ant hill. All these ants are marching along in tight formation. They're just going along and along forever, and every once in a while you see one ant that's a little farther away, out on the edge. And if he gets too far out, he's gone. He gets stepped on, or he starves to death out there by himself. But the ones that are marching in the middle aren't as interesting to me as the one that's, how can I say, out there but not getting stepped on. Almost getting stepped on—now that's fun, that's a high.

the designers

Gianfranco
Ferré,
designer, Christian
Dior

If you had locked Sophia Loren up in a closet for 20 years, what would she want to wear for her first public appearance?

In <u>Prêt-à-Porter</u>, Loren plays Isabella de la Fontaine, wife of the abhorrent, obsequious Olivier, and when he is "murdered" she's suddenly stepping out in stilettos everywhere, and the fashion pack froths up into a wild frenzy: "Isabella!" Flashbulbs popping, her giant polka-dot bow bobbing. "Isabella! Who made your dress?"

Dior, <u>naturellement</u>.

It is a historic moment in her life, the day she takes her husband's symbolically vacant seat before the eyes of the fashionable world at the prêt-à-porter shows. She is the most glamorous widow since Jackie Kennedy. A stock female character, the sexy, silk-stockinged, <u>available</u> widow definitely has A Look, and for some reason Gianfranco Ferré, the Italian design director of the very French house of Christian Dior, is an expert at it.

When it comes to mourning, Italians do it better. Add to that a little French <u>flou</u>, as they say in the workrooms of the Avenue Montaigne, and voilà: the serious black hour-glass suit, its dotted taffeta bow whooshing, up from a breathlessly delicate hummingbird throat to the oh-so-chic Jean Barthet saucer of a hat that must have blocked out three full rows behind her at every show. Amid the murmurs of admiration at the Christian Lacroix show, one photographer was heard to carp, "Ya, but it'll never fit through the emergency exit!" Gianfranco Ferré, you have created a spectacle—and a fire hazard.

Speculation swirls around the dress throughout the film. Is it a vintage Balenciaga? Vintage Dior? The Kitty Potters and Elsa Klensches of the world want to know. Says Ferré: "It is made with a pattern from my very first collection for Dior, in 1989, which was an homage to Monsieur Dior himself, his New Look, and what the house has stood for. It is a mix of femininity and sophistication. But the character, Isabella de la Fontaine, she has always been kept behind the curtains from me. They said, 'We want something to sit in the car, something to make an entrance, something to go to a funeral, to walk in the garden and be romantic.' So this is what they got.

"But dressing Isabella de la Fontaine is the same as dressing Sophia Loren," Ferré continues. "To be a great actress, there can never be a separation between creating a role and her private life." One thinks of the other great actresses of Italian cinema—Gina Lollobrigida, Claudia Cardinale, Anita Ekberg, Anna Magnani, and so on, who were stronger, stagier personalities than the characters they played. "Sophia, she goes with herself," he says in his Marlon Brando-_Godfather_ voice.

At 50, Ferré is fashion's master of the Grand Guignol, a grizzled gentleman with great cufflinks who gets into his own private jet on Wednesdays to shuttle from Milan, where he also heads his own eponymous fashion house, to Paris, where he designs the Christian Dior ready-to-wear and haute couture collections. His grandfather manufactured the famous Ferré bicycle, and he grew up in a cultivated, if severe, milieu. He eats well. He collects antique conquistador helmets and rare kepis.

"Altman is a man with power," Ferré contends. "He's a diplomat, but he has an easy way with his power over people. In all his movies his view seems so naive at the beginning, but then you see it's not like that at all." Does Ferré worry that when he finally sees Altman's fashion follies, he may think again, but to himself, "It's not like that at all"? "Doesn't matter. He's like a painter—it's how he sees it, not how we see it. That makes it more interesting."

And if Ferré himself were to make a film about fashion? "It would be more dramatic than funny," he says. "A lot more." Just then Jane Cattani, a long-ago former model who is Ferré's strikingly attractive publicist, lets out a little giggle. It seems the house of Dior is full of little dramas. She recovers quickly. It was Cattani, in fact, who brought the designer and the director together. Years ago, when Jane was working for Sonia Rykiel, Kathryn Altman, the director's wife, had expressed an interest in attending the Paris shows. She was having a hard time getting tickets, but when Cattani, an early Altman buff, got wind, she made sure there were seats, and a warm welcome, at Sonia's. Bob happened to tag along, and the rest is, as they say, history. They remained friends.

Altman uses real footage of Ferré's Dior show in Paris, as well as a snippet of a backstage interview, once again convincingly conducted by Kitty Potter for FAD-TV. "I'm standing here with the handsomest man I know," she coos. "Gianfranco, brraavisssimo!" He smiles. "You speak Italian so well!" he tells her with a straight face.

"That's how it is," he muses later, "she does it _exactly_."

Nino Cerruti: Cinema in the Buff

Speaking of Robert Altman and his take on the fashion industry, the designer Nino Cerruti said, "If you must be insulted, and from time to time you must, it's always better to be insulted by a divine woman, than by a tacky, stupid one." As he spoke, a pandemic of artificial paranoia had broken out in the Paris fashion world as Altman, The Diviner, walked freely among the designers, models, and magazine editors, two cameramen and three dozen comedic mimics in tow, at every fashion show.

To anyone who knows Altman, or Cerruti for that matter, the femaleness of that metaphor, its campy, diva sting, seems wildly out of place. Perhaps Altman, once a wry, guy's guy, has found his divinely feminine side during the making of this film, for he appears as chic and poised as a couture client. In a sense he is, having traded in his signature, slightly soiled safari suit for a complete, customized Cerruti wardrobe. Everyone who knows him talks about this change. "Now Mr. Altman is a person very, very anxious to be dressed in a certain way," Cerruti says proudly, plainly thrilled that after seeing all there is to see in fashion, Altman has picked him to wear.

Then there's the genuine article: an indisputably divine woman on the set, Anouk Aimee. The fashion collection she "designs" as the character Simone Lo is, in fact, Cerruti's collection in real life. Classic, tasteful, nice.

Cerruti is not the least bit put off by Altman's acerbic treatment of the fashion industry. "I always think that behind all irony there is always a deep love for life and a perpetual fear of

Supermodels are "a sign of a moment of weakness in fashion in which we desperately try to replace the value of the clothes with the value of the people who wear them for 20 minutes in a show."
—Nino Cerruti

being disappointed," he says of the director's work. "When Altman says he doesn't like irony, which he said at a press conference in Cannes, I think that normally you would say he's a liar. Everything he does is always full of irony. The point is that irony is not an occasional state of mind. For him, it's permanent." Cerruti hopes Altman won't spare him or his work a good healthy dose of the stuff. "It doesn't affect the value of my personal work—and beyond that, I think the world of fashion is intelligent enough to know its own quality, to know where its worth lies. But if this film will eventually have shaken out some rotten fruit, or found the worm in the apple, why not?"

Worming their way into every fancy designer apple is the fashion press, a ubiquitous federation richly represented in the film. For Cerruti, the characters played by Sally Kellerman, Tracey Ullman, Linda Hunt, Kim Basinger, Lili Taylor, and their acolytes share a sell-the-bruised-fruit-first mentality, which, he says, the press often has in real life. "There is this kind of sell-everything-short-for-the-scoop attitude," he says. "There is a lack of taste and quality not only in some of the people that make fashion but in people that cover fashion. It's a standard of quality, which has been established by television."

There is a television on every set, in nearly every scene in this movie, and inevitably, as in life, the image of a relatively new genus, the species we call supermodel, appears. Cerruti, turning wistful, says it reminds him of the final decadence of the Roman Empire. "It's a sign of a moment of weakness in fashion in which we desperately try to replace the value of clothes with the value of the people who wear them for twenty minutes in a show." Ultimately, he thinks the nude show, in which his own creations are discarded, is about "the overusage of nudity, the exploitation. That scene seems at first to stray so far from reality, but after a while you realize it's not—as Altman says, 'I don't invent anything.'"

At the film's wrap party, Cerruti asked Richard E. Grant and Sam Robards to come back to Paris and model, fully clothed, in his men's show, "because they can give the clothes the life of an actor rather than the professional work of a model."

Cerruti, a cinema buff and former milliner to Orson Welles, has done the costumes for dozens of important films. But has he ever thought about filmmaking, specifically directing? "Well, it's like if you love a woman so much you perform surgery to look inside—probably it's ugly, unpleasant, nothing to do with the beauty you admired from the outside. I don't like to go into what the French call les entrailles of a film, because you lose the myth, you kill it. There are certain realities you better not know if you want to keep on loving."

Vivienne Westwood: The Living End

"VIVIENNE IS BUMMING!"
"FASHION HITS BOTTOM!"
"WESTWOOD IN ARREARS!"
"FASHION ARSE FARCE!"

English designer Vivienne Westwood is used to this sort of silly, misguided tabloid commentary. What, you wonder, could provoke such paroxysms?

It's just a piece of plush, tufted upholstery, not unlike the velvet cushions used to display the Crown Jewels, with a lovely, squeeze-the-Charmin kind of irresistibility. You wear it, of course, on your rear end. Westwood's bubble-butt collection for fall 1994, which featured nineteenth-century-style bustles under jackets and dresses, is used, to ample effect, in Prêt-à-Porter by Altman, who has assigned it to Cort Romney, a.k.a. actor Richard E. Grant. Millions assume the director dreamed it up, to be silly. In a performance that goes over the top, Grant makes William Hurt in Kiss of the Spider Woman look like an insurance salesman.

Turn the volume down a bit, add some Bertrand Russell, a little of Aldous Huxley's Brave New World, some of John Stuart Mill's theory of the individual in society, and Westwood could be Cort Romney. She often explains her clothes through quotations. ("The tyranny of democracy is the pressure to conform.") Or as Cort Romney paraphrases, "Going back to the bustle is the only way to banish the banal, sloppy mediocrity all around us today." At any rate, she puts a lot of thought into what she does. Yet the decision to be an integral part of the film came quickly and without much quandary. "I wanted the public to see what I do, to see the clothes," she says, quite unconcerned about what Altman will do with them. "And because I'm represented as one of the three protagonist designers, my clothes have quite a big place in the film. To tell you the truth I was flattered to be one of the people representing fashion today."

Is she an Altman buff? "I haven't been to the cinema for five years, except to see <u>Dangerous Liaisons</u> twice. I don't go because I find it boring. I read books. I don't think there are any ideas in film—not that I know of, anyway—but somehow, I do remember Shelley Duvall's long legs and platform shoes in <u>Nashville</u>.

Westwood's vertiginous ten-inch platforms are now in the permanent collection of the Victoria and Albert museum in London. They've become an important part of fashion's ever-changing archaeology—one day they'll be a testament to the sexual proclivities of a vanished civilization. Over the course of a career spanning twenty-three years, Westwood has been the genesis of punk and the cynosure of the New Romantics; she has put Fragonard photoprints on corsets, made jewelry out of raw meat and matte gold male genitalia; run a shop on the Kings Road called SEX, and claims never to have had a one-night stand. These days, her clothes are very close to haute couture, in the most elegant tradition.

Vaunted by the cultural elite, she is often vilified by the press in her native England. "I could write a book about what is wrong with Westwood as a designer," snivels Colin McDowell in the (London) <u>Sunday Times</u>, "and much of it would need to be devoted to her baleful and inexplicable influence on her fellow designers." At 53, Westwood is the fashion designer's fashion designer; she's got ideas. There is every indication that in these next few years, she will finally get her due.

Richard Grant says, "Vivienne is tuned in to a different station in life, and being around her infuses the need for <u>total</u> conviction and commitment." She talked, he listened. "The first thing I told him was, 'Listen, you can't do it with just an attitude,'" Westwood says. "'You couldn't have created this collection that way.' The second was, 'I'm a woman designer—you're a man designer. You are not playing me. What I've noticed of men who love fashion is that they really want to idealize women, in a voyeuristic kind of way. You should always want to linger, to touch them that little bit longer than you should.'"

What Vivienne Westwood appreciates most in life is _effort_—taking the trouble to be sexy, to have something to say, to manage your bustle or your train or your crown in a particular way. She thinks the Queen is probably the best-dressed woman in the world. And she holds fashion models in high esteem. "For me, another very important reason for doing this film is the models—and what they _do_. These days they're the best actresses that we have, and I think people should see a lot of them. They'll do what actresses won't do anymore. I have the great reward, every six months, of seeing my work come alive, like theater, because of them, and I want people to see how committed they are."

In the film, the Cort Romney show, using Westwood's designs, takes place amid the grandeur of Château Ferrières, a Rothschild property, all clipped topiaries and Blackamoor statues. It proceeds very much like the show the designer herself had staged weeks before in the Carrousel du Louvre for the press and retailers. Here a fake-fur G-string goes under a matching fuzzy coat; there a flashing red police light serves as chapeau for a bustled Harris Tweed suit. "At one point, Richard was on camera playing with the hair before Tatiana was about to go on the catwalk," says Westwood's assistant Murray, referring to the Richard Grant character and the model Tatiana Patitz. "And I said no, no, you wouldn't do that, the hairdresser is going to do that." Westwood, who could not attend, wonders, "But was he good with the fabric? It's very spontaneous, draping. It can look a bit forced, but it's not. You're arranging the dress on the model. You're flapping about. It's very gestural, a little dancelike. It can seem theatrical." He was _very_ good with the fabric.

But fabric isn't everything. Westwood once told a reporter in Japan, "All fashion is about eventually being naked." She still thinks it's the closest anyone can come to a reasonable definition. Inevitably, the film's nude fashion show comes up. "I haven't seen it, so I don't know what it's about," she says. "But I can tell you that during my show, Kate Moss had to model a corset, which was too big for her. This could have been disastrous. It came underneath her bust, and she obviously thought it was meant to be that way—so she wore it as though she had the most beautiful dress in the world on, and that really worked. It's like a Helmut Newton photograph of a nude woman doing something domestic, as though she were wearing clothes. She's so unself-conscious. She's clothed in her nakedness. But in order to eventually be naked, you have to undress. So fashion is also about the process of undressing. I just think that a naked body will always need something—the way the Greeks had a bit of drapery on their sculpture—something that talks about the body, a pair of high-heeled shoes. Something."

Thierry Mugler: Creatures from the Fashion Lagoon

"I am the Dr. Frankenstein of fashion,"

proclaims French designer Thierry Mugler, raising his bulging left arm toward the heavens, revealing a blazing fire tattoo in the crook of his armpit.

Indeed, in his career he has created a cast of exquisite female monsters. There's the spiky, Rubberized Dominatrix, the Jungle Amazon, the Space-Age Sex Goddess, the Blue-Blooded Vampyra, the Ice-Queen Angel, the Lush-Breasted Mermaid who calls the sailors to her rocky depths—there's even a Valkyrian Biker Chic, with chrome hubcaps and five-speed handlebars protruding from her hips. These are the kind of runway clothes Mugler makes, and superbly. He sees himself as "interested only in personalities and characters, not clothes, in tricks and games and playing a role in your life." A student of acting and theater arts in college who used to see several trashy horror B-movies a day as a teen, he plays his own dangerous role convincingly: the cunning, hypermasculine Steve Reeves to Barbara Steele's campy witch in Mask of the Devil, an early favorite. If his always sexy, occasionally sinister ideas about women have been maligned by certain "important" ramparts within the press, it's hard to imagine the barbs would hurt. This is a guy who knows how to enjoy the pain, right?

Wrong. Under all that armor, Mugler is hurt, and pissed off, too. So when he was asked at his Blade Runner-style headquarters on the rue Aux Ours to discuss how he might fit into the film, he had a ready answer: "I want to say f-you to the fashion press, because they kill fashion in a way. They tend to be no makeup, gray hair, all curly and natural, flat shoes, tote-bag, beige, beige, beige. It's not fun anymore. There are no Mary Prescotts or Mrs. Maxwells or Diana Vreelands anymore. And there is nothing I hate more than the journalist who is a fake intellectual about sex and clothes."

Concentrating on the key word, "fake," one can't help but think of the Kitty Potter character, who reports for the fictional FAD-TV. With his usual flair for the dramatic, Mugler set the snare for her: An elaborate backstage scene with a writhing, shrieking group of outrageously dressed models, groupies, and dressers was painstakingly recreated in a backlot at the Carrousel du Louvre, where the Paris fashion shows are held (Mugler didn't hold a show that season). With much kissing and hysteria, we would pretend the show had just finished, and Kim Basinger, who plays Kitty Potter, would circle him in a holding pattern, "the hunter who gets captured by the game," as the old Grace Jones song goes. Her moment comes. All jitters and fake-semiotic jive, she stabs her FAD-TV mike toward his Conan pecs, and warbles on about "the overt, sexual subtext of his clothes being squarely at odds with the modern image of women as capable and independent of men." He pushes the mike away and moving closer, his hot breath on her button nose, says, "Listen, honey, fashion is all about getting a good fuck." So the unsayable—the perfect 90s fashion sound bite—has finally been said.

"I'm just worried about the camera angle," Mugler says nervously. "If the camera angle is okay, then the scene is totally real. And

Kim says, 'Oh, don't worry, just do it.' She's very sarcastic in the scene. She sees everything, she is shocked, but she also doesn't care. God, she was very, very cool."

Mugler is one of the few fashion designers who has figured out that this film is as much a satire of the press, probably more, than one of kooky clothes and their creators. "That's who should be scared, not me. They're losing power. There have never been more magazines talking about it, about fashion, but it's less and less important now. They are made by women, most of them old, who are totally against anything flamboyant or sexy. Before, in the 60s, you had a lot of art directors and editors who were men, and it was more balanced. The magazines for women are made by women, so there is only one point of view. I think it's not fair. In the 50s and 60s, because men were working on them then, the magazines were more abstract. Now everything has to be so...comfortable."

There's more: "For example, grunge. You have to think grunge to be grunge. It's not a fashion! It's an antifashion thing. So it's silly for a fashion magazine to talk and talk about it for years. It's killing the business, that's all it is. The nice girl who was grunge never ever read their magazines. She was at the flea market! She does it herself. Stupid!"

Grunge, of course, has gone the way of all fashion by now. So what's next? "Complete nudity is going to be chic, the fashion of the future," he says with the practiced air of someone who's thought about this a bit. "That's why Altman has made his nude fashion show. He sees this clearly. But you know, when everyone is nude in the streets, like the Greeks were, some kids will start up wearing Marie-Antoinette crinolines with jeans, as a reaction against bourgeois nudity, of course, and they'll probably be thrown in jail." Mugler continues with his neo-Paglian hypotheses: "And soon a woman of 60, 70, will look like 30. She'll live to be 160, 200 years old. They have already the possibility of this, with all the tricks to have a great body, all the surgery. Soon we won't need surgery either. They'll just hook you up to a machine and turn it on! That's going to be fashion—your skin! To change the skin, to make it beautiful, to change the shape."

Mugler has some ideas about cinema, too. "I've written scripts, and I've been thinking about filmmaking for a long time," he says. "I don't think what I want to do will be a commercial success, because I'm afraid it would be censored. I think that everybody wants to see it and nobody dares talk about it...I want to do porno movies!" He's out on a limb now, even for him, and he knows it. "It would be a story, with real emotions, not stupid clichés. The reality is never there. What's real is everything. I think that's why I did this thing with Robert Altman. Altman, he's real."

Lamine Kayote for Xüly Bet: Deconstructing a Real Fashion Character

HUGUES ROUSSAS PHOTOS
OF XULY BET SHOW
TO BE NEGOTIATED — NOT
EXPENSIVE.

FRANCE 42410206
123 RUE CRIMEE
PARIS 75019

At the time of <u>Prêt-à-Porter</u>'s filming, fashion had been having an <u>amour fou</u> with a curiosity called deconstruction. Simply put, that means exposed seams, unraveled hems, and recycled clothes—in other words, deconstructing the just-so look of fine fashion. It's a penitent look, we'd been told by the fashion press, designed to make us feel clean and pure and new (as opposed to junked-up and debauched and old, like all the best people in the 80s). Everywhere you looked, formerly glitzy, now plainly flagellant fashion types were literally tearing themselves up with atonement.

Enter Lamine Kayote, 31, the Senegalese designer behind the Xüly Bet label (and the model for the character Cy Bianco in the movie). Kayote had been buying cheap, nasty dresses and jackets in bulk at the tacky Paris department store Tati, ripping them apart, and recombining the ad hoc elements in hip new ways. Several seasons ago, with no money to stage a real runway show, Kayote made a big noise anyway: A school bus pulled up in front of the glazed-over gaggle of fashion folk waiting to get into the Jean-Paul Gaultier show, and thirty-two black models with boom boxes on their shoulders danced off, did fifteen minutes of funkin' with the crowd in their tight white outfits, got back on, and drove away. Shortly thereafter, the <u>New York Times</u> christened him "The Prince of Pieces," and voilà, the Funkin' Fashion Factory—his hookah-smoke-filled art-squat in an abandoned hospital far away from the fancy ateliers of the Avenue Montaigne—was super hot.

When Kitty Potter, the Southern belle reporter played by Kim Basinger, asks rival designer Cort Romney (played by Richard E. Grant), what he thinks of the deconstructed look Cy Bianco has made his name with, he is unkind. "Look," he tells her. "You cannot deconstruct a look unless you can construct one in the first place. In other words, learn to draw, then fool around with finger paints. It's what Schiaparelli said about Chanel, 'That damn bitch has been selling the same jacket for thirty-five years!' What a bore. You cannot go forward and backward. You have to go back to go forward. It's simple!"

Kayote thinks this is hilarious, even if it does make him out as a footnote to fashion history. Perhaps his moment has passed, perhaps not. But he is fearless about his decision to be in the film, and he believes and trusts in Altman. "Sometimes I get nervous about what it will reveal about me," he says, "but overall I don't care. As for the other designers, the ones who are afraid, well, that superelegant image thing is going to get ruffled. But the way they'll see it, it'll be about their own trip, their fantasy. Their whole world is built on secrets, and this film will reveal a lot and they hate that. They want a big fake enigma. Oooh, they're gonna be upset!"

What do you call those sort of stubby, shorty-style dreadlocks

that look like little feelers? Well, Lamine has them, and he's
wearing a polyester zip-front jumper with old jeans and Adidas, and
when he laughs it's so laid-back. There are graffiti all over the
walls of his workroom, and secondhand clothes sit in Everest piles
everywhere. A buyer from a big trendy California store is perched
atop one, selecting styles. Does Kayote think Altman gets this vibe?

"I saw him shooting the fashion show, my fashion show, and I said
to him, 'I think you are really into it.' I'm not big-time fashion,
I'm another kind of modern, more free and freaky, and I think the way
he improvises is very much like the way I improvise. I think I am
closer to him, to his style, and he enjoys that. There is no literal
translation of fashion. It's not fiction, this film, and it's not a
real story. It's ambiguous, in-between, and that frightens everybody
who imagines they're a part of it, whether they are or not. In the
end, Robert Altman doesn't care deeply about fashion. It's much more
interesting to look inside something than to stare at the surface,
good or bad.

"Think about the nude fashion show," he continues, referring to a
scene in the movie. "I believe it's there to make fashion think about
its ultimate goal, and that's very positive. You know, fashion can be
very out of it—like Vivienne Westwood when she puts the bum padding on
everything. There it is. You can show it. You can say it. It's there."

Lamine hastens to add that he loves what Westwood does. It is what
it is. We are living in an epoch of big, big change, he says. "It's
interesting to take a picture of it now, like an archive, which could
make this whole fashion world look really out of it."

Xüly Bet means "voyeur" in Senegalese, and the irony of that is not
lost on Kayote, as he watched Altman recreate and embellish his world.
There was Forest Whitaker, dressed just like him, nervously preening
his girls backstage in an abandoned Paris subway station, the set for
Cy Bianco's défilé, or fashion show. It was intense for Kayote.
Everything was, for him, exactly perfect. Music, makeup, sets, props,
and not least of all, Whitaker's fine performance. The actor and the
designer bonded quickly and have remained friends. "Forest put down
some lyrics for me," Kayote beams as he shifts to his next favorite
thing, music. He plays some guitar, bass, piano, and a mean harmonica.
After the day shoots, they'd jam all night, and vice versa if it was a
night call.

If he were making a film about fashion, Lamine says he'd get out of
Paris and the world of the haute couturier. "I would do something about
young vibes in Africa. I would go to the cities and just shoot." Then
he adds, humbly: "When I was an architecture student I made a three-
minute film. It was one shot, a guy and a girl, me and my girlfriend,
just being in a room, wondering what they're fucking doing together. It
was so Altman."

Sonia Rykiel: In the Beginning

I remember I had been told he was in the audience, that he had come to see the collection by chance, brought by his wife.

I remember looking at him before the collection. He had his head in his hands and was doubtless thinking of something else.

I remember when the lights lit up the runway and a woman appeared all in red, a hat firmly pulled down on her head, her hands in her pockets. And she moved forward onto the stage, glancing neither left nor right, as though she was cutting a path through space—high heels, head high, wasp-waisted—followed a moment later by three women who, for their part, seemed to be chatting among themselves and acting as if in a play.

I remember looking at him, Robert Altman, through a peephole made especially for me behind the scenery. He seemed surprised, attentive, almost enthusiastic. And then the show started and I almost forgot about him.

At the end of the show I saw him step onto the stage. He headed toward me, took me in his arms and said, "Sonia, I didn't know, I didn't imagine a fashion show could be like that. It's a film, a play. It was magnificent, I'm overwhelmed, I'll be back."

I did not believe it was true, that he would really come back, that he had been touched to the point of perhaps already having imagined a film about the fashion world. Then he really did come back. He told me, "Sonia, I'm going to make a film. I don't know when, but I'll make it." I saw him again in New York, in Paris, at rehearsals and shows. He was watching, storing up, and following everything in such a piercing, attentive way: my daughter Nathalie with her headset on for lighting, the sound, the photographers, the crowd, the frenzy, the madness, the beauty, the despair, the happiness, the fear. He created his own field, his own territory, his own story, his film. Because Prêt-à-Porter is an Altman film. It is his view of the fashion world, of the fauna of fashion, of this blend of false and true, artifice and reality, tenderness and irony.

When Picasso looked at a woman, he drew her in his own style, not as she was but as he saw her. Altman is the same. He has taken the world of fashion—the designers, the stylists, the initiated and uninitiated—at arm's length, looked at them through the eye of the camera, and this has become Prêt-à-Porter. As he did with Short Cuts and The Player and all the others.

He is an immense creator, a fantastic actor, and a terrific director.

I love him because he is the first filmmaker to have seen all the intense work that makes a fashion show. I love him because he has put his finger on this baroque and bizarre world, so touching, so full of love for fashion. I love him because he has kept his word: two years ago he said "I'm going to make this film" and he made it. I love him because like all the "great" men, he makes use of everything, he overrides everything, but he pursues his objective above and against all. I love him because he sometimes seems vague, but his ideas are well-established.

I don't know whether the finished film Prêt-à-Porter will be exactly what he had in mind, but I fancy that such is often the case. What I do know is that for me, this film is magical, that I am proud and happy to have been the starting point of this story, and that this experience will remain one of the most magnificent of my life.

st

the stars

Sophia Loren:

On Bob: "I like the way the light shines in his eyes." "We don't do it for the money. People like him don't grow on trees." "Marcello and I recreated a scene from a movie we did years ago called Yesterday, Today and Tomorrow, with De Sica. It's very amusing, filled with bubbles. I do my strip tease for Marcello and he howls just like he did in the first movie, except in that one he was ready to make love and in this one he falls asleep! He was impotent because, you know, it was cold in Russia. That was his alibi! He was no tiger, not like the first movie."

"Kim Basinger introduced me to her father, and I thought, now she's my girl. What a nice family. She's my girl." — Kim.

"I love my clothes, but I don't care for them." "I don't know if I will watch the nude show when the film comes out. I don't know why. The idea is great, the symbolism is great, but I am shy about it. I won't like to see it. Maybe that's why it's good."

SER GEÏ OBLOMOV
Marcello
Mastroianni

MOSCOW
Se 1
cost ①

Dark
colors

lunettes du costume piqué
à Danny Aiello.

Rubber
snow boots
+ zip.

Marcello Mastroianni: "Anouk Aimée talking on the right, Sophia Loren talking on the left, what can I do?"

Linda Hunt: "In Paris last winter I learned that Cole Porter was right. It does drizzle in Paris in the winter. (Springtime? Which is it?)"

"Peter Bray played my son, Oxblood Oxheart, in <u>Popeye</u> with Bob, and Pete is a man of gargantuan proportions. The two of us standing together are like the grain of sand and infinity. When Bob first introduced us all I could think was, 'Oh my God, how is this possible? How could I have given birth to big Pete?' I said something like that to Bob. He thought a moment and said, 'It must have been a pretty long labor.'"

"The most important fashion icon in all of film history is the ruby slippers in <u>The Wizard of Oz</u>. Neither clever nor amusing, they simply underline the importance of wearing just the right shoes when you travel."

Anne Canovas:

"Bob said: 'I want a strange couple where you look a little bit alike. You are Cort's muse. A little masculine, androgynous, in charge of the business part too. He is the artist. You are in love with the boyfriend of his boyfriend [Cy Bianco], but secretly.'"

"I learned, on the set, that the way you look at others in the film is more important than what you say."

"Working with Bob is wildly exciting, backbreakingly difficult, and spiritually uplifting, but never absurd."

Tara Leon:

"Bob said he wanted Kiki to be jaded, messy, frazzled, and definitely affected by the business. So, that's what I gave him.

"To me, if you dress, you're a cross-dresser."

"I've always thought Bob was a genius from before I met him, and from this experience I found him to be a kindred spirit as well."

"Fashion sucks one season and is fabulous the next. It pays my rent and obviously it affects the way I live. The nude scene said flesh is best. I would guess God's the best designer."

"The most difficult thing for me was walking down the runway completely naked, where humiliation and vulnerability ran deep. Usually on a runway it's more a case of being overdone. This scene was raw—the naked truth!"

Georgianna Robertson:
"Basically, I am the good sister."

"Some people have problems handling fame, sudden fame, or even problems with fame before fame arrives! In contrast to real stars like Sophia Loren who to my surprise turned out to be open, friendly, and very supportive."

"Danny Aiello's shaved legs would make any woman jealous, to the extent that they even seemed to make an experienced man like Robert Altman nervous!"

"The nude fashion show says, 'What's all the fuss about $10,000 dresses that show more skin than they cover?'"

"I was forced to make the choice between canceling a cover shoot for a magazine or shooting the scene where I have a cat fight with my sister on the runway. So instead, I started the fight the day before at the rehearsal. Bob didn't know, the crew didn't know, just my 'sister' knew I was gonna do this. There was no mattress because it was unplanned, so a scar on my knee is my permanent souvenir of the film. I shot the cover the next day too."

Julia Roberts:
You get a little sketch, and you have to color it in. Bob gave Tim and I a map of this journey and we went! I've never had this much fun shooting a film before.

Tim and I would have lunch and he'd say OK, so what are we going to do today? We didn't know! We had this not terribly original story—boy meets girl, boy fucks girl, boy loses girl—and so we tried to make it kookier and funnier in very subtle ways and very, very silly ways. It's like, his fly is open and my pants are down to my knees—most people won't even notice but we thought it was hysterical. Bob trusts that you don't have to 'milk it.' You can't get much sillier than making out through a sheet while imitating Casper the Friendly Ghost, but we did that like we meant it! We were so off our heads! I did some things that were so wacky they're stupid. I don't think I could have really done this with someone who I wasn't good friends with—Tim Robbins and I are very good friends. There were times, sitting in a room with Bob Altman and Tim Robbins—two men I have such respect and admiration for—that I'd think, 'What am I doing here?' They are both so funny, so brilliant. But you press on. You have guts and you say, 'Oh, but this will be funny, or let's try that.' You have to shoot from the hip. Playing drunk and giggly can be badly done. But with Anne Eisenhower, all her defensiveness, the bravado of being a woman in a 'career' turns into the opposite, and she's deeply silly with a drink in hand. She's actually funny."

Stephen Rea:
"When people of genius invite you to work with them you should immediately accept."

"Bob said to me, 'I see this as a series of explosions, with a thin black sizzling line running through. Milo is the thin black line.'"

"I'm sitting in the audience and the camera is rolling and Steven Meisel is sitting across from me and therefore I cannot be Steven Meisel. Steven, I met him in New York once, he's a nice guy and the thing is Milo is not a nice guy."

"You want to know the truth? I never looked at fashion magazine pictures until this. I looked at them a lot, now I don't look at them again anymore."

"I like it, fashion, I understand something about it, but I know nothing about it."

"I find shopping for a character much easier than shopping for myself."

"I think I'll never see a better scene than Marcello singing while he sewed his suit with the little portable sewer."

Rupert Everett: "I hustled myself into this film. I suddenly realized if I wasn't in it it would be the end of my career because I'd have no excuse for living in Paris anymore if I wasn't in it."

"I said to Bob that I should really be in the film and he agreed and I got a little role, which then got bigger."

"I've been around fashion a lot. It's a world that makes me laugh. I was a model."

"Lauren Bacall, I really like her. She's a fantastic monster!"

Lauren Bacall:
"Slim Chrysler is the grande dame, the guru, the woman with the taste and power."

"Steven Meisel looks terribly bored at the shows to me."

"Elegant? What does it mean anymore?"

"I knew Diana Vreeland well. She's the one who put me on the cover of <u>Harper's Bazaar</u>. She wrote a little something about me that said 'actress' because she knew that's what I wanted to be. She was a terrific woman. I'm certainly not playing her. Nobody could be Diana Vreeland but Diana Vreeland."

"I totally trust Altman. My life is in his hands."

"The gloss of life doesn't interest him and I don't think fakery is high on his agenda."

"So basically, we came to Paris to a c t stupid and be silly?"
—Julia Roberts

1) Who in Hell is Kitty Potter? Describe her!

(1) Kitty is:

A - a FORMER WEATHER girl FROM a local T.V. station in TEXAS.

B - FORREST GUMP in dESiGNER clothes getting her instructions FROM Ads in FASHION MAGAZINES that READ London PARIS Hambury PalmspRings.

C - and most of all - SOMEONE I would have loved to smother with a pillow during the MAKING of this picture.

2) What is it about Bob? Everybody says he gives you your freedom, he lets you make mistakes— can you go beyond that, or get more personal?

(2) A - He's the last one to show up FoR the pokER gAME and the only one who doesn't cheat but he leads the others to think he does ——

B - Without letting it get out of hand, he's the kind of MAN who would let the help steal FROM the till EVERY ONCE IN A while because he KNOws its good FoR the MORALE and you get MORE work out of them —

C - HE has AlwAYS possessed a STATE of the art bullshit dETECTER (NASA built) As a director AND As a human being —

B-CON'T SAME with ACTORS — he lets EVERYONE think they ARE So good that they NEEd NO direction, just aFEW MINOR sugestions FROM him — That is why actors FEEl So FREE when working with him ———— THEN! —— he gets the pERFoRMACE he wANTS WHEN he Edits and you (the actoR) NEVER rEMEMBER HAVing done half the stuff he got you to do.

C — HE is Also VERY SECURE in his cho. of actors for the roles in his films HE SEES through the PERSON and KNOW'S what they ARE CAPABLE of doing and oR. bRINGING to the SCREEN in the role THE physical surface is NEVER a deterent HooRAy FOR ME !!!!!!)
HE'S BRAVE and so Much FUN !!

3) Bob and Scotty have both told me how much they respect you—using (as an example of who you are) the time you 'gave it to Bob' on the set of Fool For Love when he accused you (wrongly) of being a prima donna. Can you tell it, and explain your relationship with Bob?

(3) HE BECAME A VERY iNfluENTiAl MAN iN My liFE OVER That iNcidENT — I ~~Nevel~~ FEll iN love with him — FrOM ThEN ON I wANTED him to bE psou OF ME and the WOrk hE and I WERE doi A MAN AS big and rEVERED as hE iS admitting HE WAS WRONG? That you SEldom EXPERiENCE if EVER iN this busiN. It also helped test My Ability to stand u FOR MySElF — A lot was accomplished thaiNight.

4) Tell me your feelings about the 'Cher at the Bulgari party' scene. (PS— it's cut brilliantly and really works.)

(4) FrightMARE ! — I AlwAyS wANTED to MEET ChER but NOT likE that.

5) And the Elsa Klensch scene? (how she threw out text last minute...).

(5) ANothER FrightMARE ! AltMAN had FuN throwing ME to the wolVES ~~from~~ FrOM TiME to TiME — I heard, that aftER the iNTERVIEw shE told SOMEONE iN A MAGAZiNE I wAs swEET but didN't KNOW the First thing About FASHiON — NOt ONly wAs shE right, but I thought a dECONStructiONist WAs SOMEONE who tORE dOWN houses — yEt I thiNK I got hER with SNOOp DOggy Dô ShE didN't hAVE a CluE.

6) What do you think the film's about?

(6) I DON't KNOW.

7) What's the nude show for, in your opinion, and what is Kitty Potter's "I HAVE HAD IT!!" speech about there?

(7) I WAS SO glad shE got to rEliEVE hERSElf OF hERSElf and all CONCERNED — I actually FElt ON COMMON ground with hER that night — ENough WAS ENough THE MOViE — THE GlAMOUR THE FlashbulbS — April iN PARis THE Bullshit — THE hotel

The Crowds and the OCCENT
and idiotic characterization
I MADE up to do this job
It WAS independence day
for ME 🇺🇸 ▓ After that Night
I WAS in bed in the hotel in PAR
with the flu (the vomiting and diarrhea kind
Kitty Potter gave ME A virus!

8) What do you imagine Kitty Potter will do after renouncing fashion? Just fantasize about her new life if the film continued.

(8) She went back to school and becomes a veterinarian / marine biologist

9) Can you think of a 'fashion moment' from any old movie that you loved? I'm asking everybody this, and I've got answers like-- "when Scarlet O'Hara makes the curtains into a dress", or "when Jaye Davison takes of her silk slip in The Crying Game and she has a dick!", etc, etc. Pick anything you like.

(9) When Scout wore the HAM suit in "To Kill A Mocking Bird" - It was a brilliant MOMENT in fashion MANEUVERING Around in that suit took Alot of skill in those Dark Woods

10) How was Chiara?

11) The Barbara Walters Question: If Kitty Potter were a dog in the dog fashion show at the beginning of the movie, what breed would she be, and what would she want to be wearing?

(10) Chiara is beautiful smart and extremely funny Not to mention sensitive and As talented As she ~~chooses~~ chooses to expose - I love her and could not have had a better assistant -

I miss you Brian - the questions were great!
Love
Kim

Lili Taylor: "The shows made me sad at times; they were a bit robotic."

"Fiona is very identified with her lesbianism; she's never doubted who she was. There is no internalized homophobia. She's not a butch haircut with a tool belt, she's not this stereotypical idea of a lesbian, and my lesbian friends are happy about that."

"Journalists have to be strong, mentally, physically, they have to put up with a lot of big egos. Trying to get an interview for them is like cat-and-mouse. People get supercilious and aloof, it's hard. But Fiona would rather go in in a softer way. She relies on her eyes, her kindness, instead of a super-predator manipulation."

"The nude show is sublime, because you have all these people with their own agendas, creating insanity, which jeopardized one woman, Simone Lo, her heart and soul, until she took the power her own way. Very sublime."

Ute Lemper: "Before shooting, he was scared he wouldn't show enough, then he was scared my water would break any minute! I was too! I mean, I was ready..."

"First, you see the belly. And that's such a secret and wonderful shape, only women who have the privilege of experiencing it can know how I felt on the runway, because I was so proud. Very, very proud. Besides, you couldn't see anything because the belly was covering it all up!"

"I would have liked a zoom close-up on the belly. But the other girls were beautiful nude too, as you know, and that's the point."

"I'm the boss. They're not the boss. I say what is good about me, my clothes don't.".

"I am very happy that this send-up of this very absurd, totally perverse, and ridiculous world now exists."

"A naked pregnant woman is about many things, but sex isn't one of them."

"Lauren Bacall is very funny—a totally sarcastic woman, I love her speaking her French! Pardonnez-moi, and all that, she's a real cookie."

"This film is about dancing on the volcano."

Danny Aiello: "Do I look like a young Lauren Bacall?", (in drag) "I was driving from Jersey into the city when I got a call from Bob, he was in Paris, callin' me on my car phone and I say, hello? And he says to me Danny, I'm finally gonna bring you outta the closet." "I have a newfound respect for women, just for high heels alone. I practiced for two weeks alone, in my hotel room at night. People across the street loved it." "I'm like the last heterosexual, a very macho guy. To have my fans accept me like this, running around in a dress and a wig, I got concerned. You can see I'm a macho guy!

"I'm a fan of the fashion industry—it has intelligence and talent."

Personal Diary of Richard E. Grant

Tuesday 8th March, 1994

The crew are shooting another show and I am ushered to a front-row seat for Chantal Thomas's lingerie collection. What follows is forty minutes of turbocharged teenage fantasia with underwear invention beyond the preconceptions in my head. Cher slips into the vacant seat beside me as the lights dim. She is dressed top-to-toe in leather designed by Chrome Hearts. She looks like Cher and having read her age cannot detect a line to declare anything more than late thirties. No sooner has she sat down than the whisper is out and lenses redirect themselves and click.

The working actors are back at the makeshift "backstage" and getting undressed and sorting out dinner plans. Lauren Bacall has invited a bunch of us to her favorite Chinese restaurant and Monsieur Pierre, chief talent scout from Elite Model agency, is here to ask if I will have dinner with Naomi Campbell, Kate Moss, Johnny Depp, and Christy Turlington at Natasha's Restaurant, followed by a party for Naomi at Le Palais club. In the name of "research" I opt for the latter. Forest Whitaker is also invited and we taxi out into the Paris night for a dose of the supermodel lifestyle. They are an hour late, delayed by the last show, which makes little difference as the food they order is mostly played with and pushed around the plate and I wonder whether they ever eat anything. Naomi assures us that she eats like a horse. About four jumbo packs of Marlboros are inhaled between details about who is with whom and who is in town and what happened at this show and what freebie was doled out to so and so and these perfectly beautiful creatures seem <u>so</u> young. I am, at the age of 36$\frac{1}{2}$ feeling like an

ancient elder. It's the readjust of being with humans <u>born</u> in 1974 and stalling any conversation about "Remember that scene in <u>The Godfather</u>" kind of talk. I wonder what value they place on anything when it seems that for the hallowed few, constant adulation, presents, attention, mobiles, cars, suites at the Ritz and the clothes and jewels from the designers render forking out their <u>own</u> money a novelty. How do you avoid being spoilt? How do you face the day when the next bright young find edges you out? There are obvious similarities with the star-thesp, but in the scheme of things modeling does not have the tag of real talent attached or much prospect of longevity. But if you are scheduled to fly to the Bahamas in between London, Paris, and New York all the time, this does not loom as a priority. They assure my skeptical query that the "girls" are incredibly supportive of one another and not bitchy at all and it would take armor plating not to be charmed by their sheer form: so rich, so young, so tall and so thin.

But what to really talk about crossed my wires amid the fury of names and places being exchanged like so many cents. I wondered at the crossover of pop music and supermodels, both leading travel-full, moneyed, peripatetic lives and being in each other's videos. Naomi is in the middle of recording an album and has written a book and it seems every feature is a possible commodity.

I never saw money anywhere and when it came time to go, all was <u>taken care of</u>. As I hardly knew any of them, felt somewhat embarrassed, said so and was assured <u>not</u> to. We have had the center table and given the other punters a free show of sorts.

Johnny Depp, whom I first met when he was with Winona Ryder and still bears her name tattooed on his shoulder, is apparently possessed of Kate Moss and they look like brother and sister blowing smoke into each other's faces between kisses. The all-change-at-Charing-Cross-station syndrome of romance never ceases to wobble my brain, and I couldn't help compare the man I had met on the set of <u>Dracula</u> with Winona, with this incarnation as escort to a supermodel.

To the Palais Club where a party is being given in honor of Naomi and I haven't been in such a cave since I hung up my platforms and flares in the 70s, and spy many girls dressed in the very hipsters and clonking shoes and bells that defined that decade as the worst possible taste. Grab your fast-shifting youth, boy, and "bang shang a lang boof" and just hope to hell no one espies you through the smoke haze making a complete gonad of yourself. Naomi pays me the compliment that I <u>can</u> dance, having clearly anticipated the Prince Charles School of Rhythm and Blues and I bleat forth some inanity about having grown up in Africa. This seems to explain.

I lurch out into the freezing air, past the crush of eagers desperate to get inside, past the chunks of bodyguard. Naomi, Linda, Helena chorus up like a desperate plea as we scram into the cars and I can go home to savor the fast lane of a Paris night with the fast folk.

Phone messages from home slipped under my door in crisp white envelopes and spelling out sweet nothings. "You are old Father William the young man said and yet you still stand upon your head?"

3 A.M. and out.

Wednesday 9th March

In the name of research, I am ticketed into more shows, the first being Valentino and I am seated beside Jackie Collins and Rupert Everett. Rupert was as skinny as myself and I amazed at his physical transformation: his arms now being thicker than my thighs and neck as wide as his jaw. "Gym ever day." "Why?" "Sex." Touché.

The now expected delay before the show starts gives ample time to instantly get to know your famous neighbor, while ignoring the clicking zooms that have suddenly honed in, and will drone elsewhere in a nanosecond when some alternative creature appears.

Jackie, as she insists on being called, is funny, disarming, and has the effect of making you feel as if you have known each other forever. Rupert further proves himself to be the ubiquitous Englishman Abroad and knows her already and is plugging for tips on how to write a novel.

Diane Von Furstenburg sits as the lights go down and again all is friendly, bright, and beautiful.

In with the models, despite who having been up all hours, seem serenely unaffected by no sleep. I know I am not twenty.

Mr. Valentino's clothes are greeted with outbursts of applause and much nodding, oohing and aahing from an appreciative, solidly pleased crowd. He struts down the runway, surrounded by the applauding models and seems the most comfortable in this starring role of the designers yet seen. Sleek, suntanned, coiffed, and I am whispered has had a good face job. The scram for the nearest exit or backstage homage ensues and Jackie is off and I shuffle into the adjoining salle for Yves Saint Laurent's show. Catherine Deneuve entered shortly before the lights went down and unlike any of the other celebrities, her status here seems nothing short of royal.

Altman's open invitation to watch the dailies is the closest equivalent to the binding process of rehearsal. You get to see everyone else's work, go out together, and though you may be one of twenty character parts, it goes a long way in explaining how the overall acting style is so homogenous. Ensemble play abolishes the usual hierarchy of director, stars, and spear carriers. The director is undeniably omnipotent in terms of the final version but you feel that the actor-crew response is the unfinished film's first audience and the response to whether a scene works or not is naturally going to be that much more critically judged in this safe house and will affect the editing. Likewise it offers the opportunity for people to enjoy takes that never make it to the final version and there is always an all-right-on-the-night blooper to remind perfectionists of their fallibility. An audience at once supportive and Sweeney Todd cutthroat. Playing a character is inevitably somewhat myopic and seeing yourself operating in the context of everyone else is helpful and informative. Plus, you get to go out for dinner afterwards! As a result it is an antidote to the usual film experience whereby you can feel isolated if you don't work every day, as the dailies become a meeting point. American actors constantly quote working with Altman as like being at summer camp. The unspoken trust and the opportunity to really contribute returns you to when you started acting and it being the raison d'être for getting up every day. More than this it would seem churlish to ask for. Not that this is all rosy-glosy hold hands and sigh <u>aah</u>! In every company there are inevitably going to be one or two prize arseholes and this one is no exception.

As we are all in such close proximity and given free reign to improvise, offer and invent stuff, the competitive quotient is high and the egos a yo-yo-ing, which perfectly mirrors the tightly wrapped fashion world we are imitating.

We are given verbal invites to a club L'Arc situated off the Arc de Triomphe in honor of Cher, who is in town for the shows and Chrome Hearts, the leatherwear designers from L.A. she favors. Naomi, Kate, and Johnny are due and we drop the right names at the door and are reluctantly let inside. Tracey Ullman immediately senses our lowly status and ripostes with the observation that we are in a Euro-trash crowd. I assume this covers the gamut of people of all ages as opposed to those born in the 70s, most of whom are overcoiffed and bedecked in Versace or imitation gold chain, earrings, and links. Word filters through that there is a roped-off area deeper within that we might be privileged to and we crush thither past buffet tables laden with almost bleeding beef. We foolishly get a leg over the rope but are stopped mid-straddle by bodyguards who rattle off in Franglais about exclusif pour les stars. Bollocks. It is like being a teenager unable to get into an 18-certificate film again. None of us is particularly keen to be here in the first place and now it's two g's in <u>bugger off</u> time. Naomi, Kate, Johnny, and Cher burrow through and it's ropes away. At which point our lack of global recognizability has taken its toll and we retire to the Val d'Isere for some food.

I find a Chanel invite, care of Naomi, at the hotel for the following morning.

Thursday 10th March

Kate and Naomi invite Tracey Ullman and I to brunch at the Ritz Hotel. Tally ho. An incredible stuffed-seat plush palace with adjoining conservatory garden is our rendezvous. A plethora of waiters and elderly rich folk filing in for prelunch cocktails and canapés. Naomi arrives in eyeball-swiveling lingerie that could be comfortably packaged in a matchbox, inducing near-fatal thrombotics from the old prostates in pinstripe. Kate is mini-skirted by a white lace child-sized shirt tied at the side, with a bare midriff and tiny vest. Johnny Depp, in trademark just-outta-bed-denim-and-Dean look, is stopped by the maître d'. There is a tie and jacket dress code altercation and within two seconds voices are crescendoing at which point Naomi legs up and charms things down. The result is waiter revenge; getting breakfast and drink is a battle. Travel plans were the conversationals alongside the waiter-war now being waged. Kate was off to St. Bart's for a shoot, Naomi to Dublin to see her fiancé and all the eggs Florentine and Perrier and champagne signed to a room number and yet again no money was seen or changed human hands.

This is the finale of real-life research time, and my first proper filming call is scheduled for early evening at a famed restaurant in the gardens near the Place de la Concorde. Jeweler Bulgari is the party host in conjunction with the film production.

This is true Armani-ism, real-life and reel-life, with a bona fide event interweaved with film actors playing characters attending the kind of party usually created in a film studio. The entrance is a red carpet and candle-lit extravaganza with the name Bulgari on a framework of mini-candles. Part of the restaurant is requisitioned for the actors. I do not expect to see Sophia Loren and Marcello Mastrioanni chatting to one another in dressing gowns and hair curlers. But they are. And then it's a go-round of howdy-doody to Kim, Tracey, Stephen, Danny, Rupert, Lauren, Sam, Lily, Ute, Lyle, Forest, Chiara, Rossy, Sally, Linda, Michel, and Anouk.

All the usual separate caravan/dressing-room-suite hierarchicals are dispensed with and you know that you are unmistakably on an Altman. And he is in there giving ideas and suggestions to each and everyone and checking what everyone is wearing and going to be doing. The closest experience to this communal dressing room camaraderie I have experienced was many years ago working in a fringe theater company. Except that you don't remember sitting next to Lauren Bacall discussing the state of Ya. Bob Altman announces that the night will be long and declares that he hasn't a clue as to exactly what will or won't happen, but to all hang in there and that everyone who has dialogue will be covered by one or other camera. It is with some trepidation that I get my Vivienne Westwood gear on, as it is the first outing in the film and the look is at its most extreme for this particular scene. The eighteenth-century white makeup, beauty spot, and kiss-curl Marcel-waved hair help me to feel "hidden," before strapping into the crotch-high black boots with the

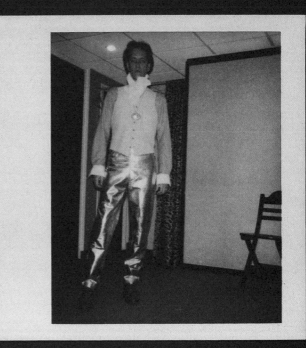
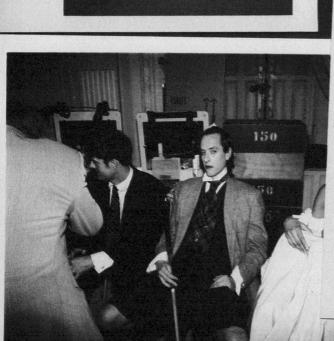

twelve-inch heels, dinner jacket, hat, pearl earring, and gold penis cufflinks. Plus a floor-length velvet double-breasted coat. A very deep breath before sallying forth into the critical eye storm of the other thesps. Lauren Bacall is guffawing her disbelief while others offer approval, especially La Loren, which is no small encouragement at this point. In order not to fall off the heels, I have been provided with an elaborate billiard cue which serves as a walking stick. Helmut Newton, the legendary German lensman and leather _obsessif_, is here to cover the night and is muchly taken with the sheer endless length of my Westwood boots. Once costumed and bouffed, we are trooped off in small groups to be mixed into the party. A Liquorice All-Sorts of minor Euro-royalty, counts and socialites of every age and type, real designers and supermodels and filmstars flitting through Paris and, it seems, this movie. One of whom is Cher, ageless in tight leather and waist-length hair who asks whether I know Rupert Everett or not? Elsa Klensch, fashion editor of CNN news, sets up an interview with me "in character," which induces a minor coronary palpitation, having yet to _do_ anything in the movie as such. This is a one-to-one in depth about the fashion philosophy of Cort Romney, the designer I am playing. Having spent some time absorbing Westwood at firsthand, I intone with as much sincerity as I can muster, just _why_ and _what_ and _wherefore_ it all means and leads.

I meet up with Vivienne Westwood, who wholly endorses the character before her, and I feel that her endorsement at this point is as important as Mr. Altman's. Even the briefest encounter with Vivienne leaves you in no doubt that she is a true original and unlike anyone else. Listening without apparent preconceptions, she seems curious and open to whatever is going on, which is then filtered and reconstituted through her own unique take on things.

WRAP. 1 A.M. And a scramble out and off to Les Bains Douche club where the finale of the season is being celebrated. There are crowds outside: bouncers, poseurs, drunks, bikers, wannabees, models, et al. We are told to drop supermodel passwords to get through the human crush and squelch through barrier of garlic fume and pit to get into the smoke-smogged interior that divides into upstairs bar/restaurant and downstairs dance floor. Up we congo and pass Jackie Collins who greets us as if we are the oldest friends, along to the back tables where reside the beauteous young and rich. Simon Le Bon and Mick Hucknall are to be espied. It suddenly seems a small city in that everyone we seem to have met since arriving is now somewhere in this building before being flung to some far distant island for a shoot or publicity trail. Rupert declares that this crowd is too "boringly hetero-bourgeois" and kilts off into the night.

4 A.M. and to bed.

MIRAMAX BOOKS
DELILAH BOSANQUET

BRIAN I HOPE YOU CAN UNDERSTAND MY ENGLISH CONSTRUCTION, IF I MADE   A
MISTAKES OR IF YOU DON'T UNDERSTAND SOMETHING PLEASE CALL ME. I ENYOY VERY MUCH
THE INTERVIEW AND YOUR FUNNY QUESTIONS. GOD LUCK WITH THE BOOK AN THANKYOU
FOR CALLING ME.

HERE ARE THE ANSWERS:

1+ BOB TOLD ME THAT PILAR WAS SIMONE LO(ANOUK AIMEE)'S FIRST ASISTANT, A
BECAUSE SIMONE LO HAS A LOT OF PROBLEMS PILAR TRIES ALL THE TIME TO MAKE

THE THINGS EASIEST TO HER. THE CLOTHES PILAR WORNS IN THE MOVIE ARE SO
FUNNIES AND SHE ALWAYS SHOW HER LEGS. PILAR IS A VERY TENDER WOMAN WHO
TRIES TO SURVIVE IN HER HARD WORK(SHE SUPERVISES EVEYTHING IN SIMONE LO'S
ATELLIER)AND HAVE FUN AT THE SAME TIME.

2- I KNEW THAT REALITY AND FICTION CAN BE VERY CLOSE IN CINEMA BUT
I NEVER SAW THAT BEFORE IN THE WAY THIS REALITY AND FICTION MIX IN PRET A
PORTER - AS A CORAL FILM WE HAVENT ENOUGH TIME TO COMPOSE THE CHARACTERS
WE MUST TO GIVE TO THE CARACTER A LOT OF PERSONAL THINGS AND THE RELATI
ONSHIPS WE HAVE DONE TO EACH OTHERS WAS ALWAYS A MIX BETWEEN OUR OWNS
PERSONALITYS AND CARACTERS ONES.

3- BOB IS FIFTY GOD AND FIFTY DEVIL HE DOESNT EMIT JUDGEMENTS, HE PUTS
ALL THESE PEOPLE TOGETHER AND LETS THEM FREE TO CRATE TO FEEL WELL OR BAD
(IT IS UP TO THEM), AND HE "ONLY" FOTOGRAPHS THIS CRAZY MIX WITH ALL THE
CONSEQUENCES. AS A MAN BOB IS IRRESISTIBLE, NOBODY MAN OR WOMAN CAN SAY
NO TO HIM; HE HAS STRONG CARISMA AND AN ENORMUUS POWER OF SEDUCTION. HE
IS A MATURE MAN WITH AN IPRESSIVE BACKGROUND AT THE SAME TIME HE HAS THE
FRESHNESS AND ENERGY OF A BOY BEGINNING HIS LIFE EVERY DAY. I LOVE HIM.

4- I AM IN IT AND OUT OF IT AT THE SAME TIME, I THINK THIS IS THE BETTER
WAY TO LOOK AT FASHION. THE NUDE FASHION SHOW IN THE FILM WAS A TERRIFIC
EXPIRIENCE, SO MAGIC, SO TENDER AND ROMANTIC, WE FEEL SO FREE AFTER DO IT.
FOR ME THIS IS THE MESSAGE FREEDOOM, FREDOOM TO CHOSE.

5- I COULD KILL FOR EVERY SINGLE DRESS WORN BY ALL WOMEN CHARACTERS IN
FELLINI'S LA DOLCE VITA. IT S SIMPLY TOO MUCH. WHERE DAMN ARE ALL THOSE
DRESSES GONE?

6- A BLACK DOGO WITH A TURBANT(MADE WITH A BLUE JEANS T SHIRT) ON HIS
HEAD AND A FALSES DIAMOND COLLIER.

7- NO ESPECIFIC ENEMY! MY CHARACTER'S WORST ENEMY AND BEST FRIEND ARE
LIFES CIRCUNSTANCES. JUST LIKE ME.

8- THIS FILM IS ABOUT LIFE IN THE CRAZY WORLD OF FASHION, AND AS IT
COMES OUT SUPERFICIAL THINGS AND DEEP ONES ARE MUCH MORE CLOSER THAN WE
THINK: YOU JUST HAVE TO READ BETWEEN LINES AND NOT STOP AT FIRST LOOK.
   THERE ARE A LOTS OF EXCITING AND ABSURD THINGS TO TELL YOU BUT I AM
A "PETIT COMITE GIRL": I LAUGHED, I WORKED, I LEARNED, I MADE A ~~GRERT~~ GREAT
FRIENDS, I LOVED A LOT OF PEOPLE, I CRIED LIKE A BABY WHEN EVERYBODY
CLAPPED ME AT THE END OF MY ROLE, I HAD THE MOST FUN OF MY LIFE AND AS
BOB SAID ~~TO~~ ALL OF US IN THE FIRST MEETING: "IF THIS MOVIE IS GOOD
EVERYTHING WILL BE OKEY, IF IS BAD EVERYTHING WILL BE BETTER THE ONLY
THING WE HAVE TO DO IS RELAX AND HAVE FUN" AND HAVING FUN IS REALLY
WHAT I DONE : THANKYOU BOB YOU MADE ME SO HAPPY.

Rossy de Palma (signature)

P.P. DELILAH. I WILL BE HERE IN ITALY
UNTILL 10 SEPTEMBRE. IF YOU NEED SOMETHING
ELSE CALL ME PLEASE. KISSES.

Brau,

MET NUMBER IS 3943968
OOO

ROOM 311.

(initial)

The Bulgari party as seen by Helmut Newton

grand
+ sac vert

These conversations, between Marcello Mastroianni and his daughter (with Catherine Deneuve), Chiara Mastroianni, and between Lauren Bacall and her son (with Jason Robards) Sam Robards, happened on the set, during the Bulgari party at the restaurant Le Doyen in Paris. This was the first time both of the younger actors had worked alongside their parents.

Marcello Mastroianni: The light is not good there, don't sit there.

Chiara Mastroianni: I don't mind.

M: I'm just thinking, for your career—my career is OK, so you should think about yours.

C: OK, we'll change places. I don't know what to ask you. Help me!

M: I don't want to give away the story of the movie. We should let the director do that. If I was a director doing interviews, I'd always tell the press a different story. I'd make things up like crazy.

C: You're right. They show too much on TV and in magazines.

M: But sometimes the documentary on the making of the film is better than the film. You get to go backstage, all that. Some films, that's better.

C: How do you think Altman can gather so many actors together to do little parts?

M: His charisma, his professional reputation, his way of working—he's a great director. It's a big chance for any actor, even just for one or two days to be a part of this film. He's an artist.

C: You said you like to come in the morning with absolutely no idea of what you'll do that day. Why?

M: Listen, it's a boring job. You wait all day for ten hours, then work one hour, the other nine you're sitting. So to have a surprise is better. It was like that with Fellini. I know the idea they have, I know the character I'm playing, and I react. I can surprise myself that way. I don't like to prepare too much. You get totally prepared, and the director asks for something different! Your character speaks in your head, like a cricket.

C: A cricket?

M: OK, not a cricket. Anyway, I will ask you questions now. How did you feel when Altman called?

C: I was so excited, I really couldn't believe it. I called you, remember?

M: Yes, and you had a complex, remember? You thought I arranged this, but I didn't. Acting is the only job where you can't recommend your kid. If you're a minister, you can recommend your son to be a minister. An actor can't. Unless the director is very bad.

C: Yes, but it was too good to be true!

M: And now that the movie is almost finished?

C: I'm so sad. I know you are getting sad too because it's almost all over.

M: Yes. It's a family, each film. It's like going to camp. Everybody does some different sport, and you say "see you next summer, let's write, let's call," and it never happens. Now you must think of the next movie.

C: The party is over.

M: I had the same experience as this one with Fellini. It's a wonderful circus.

C: It's eleven-thirty and I still haven't shot my scene. I think we're finished for today.

M: But you interviewed me! You haven't lost your day, don't think so badly of me! We should stop because now we are boring.

C: Everybody talks and talks so much about this film—is there anything left for them to say when it comes out?

M: I know. Are you going home now?

C: Yes.

M: I'll give you a lift.

Sam Robards: This is so strange! Why are you here?

Lauren Bacall: Altman. Number one, he's brilliant. He has a definite concept. He has tremendous taste, he loves actors, it's fun, it's ensemble work, not a bunch of people who want to get out front and take it all for themselves. You know this won't be mediocre. And let's face it, most of the work we do as actors is mediocre.

S: How has this experience been?

L: Tiring! Very long hours, we don't always know what's what. We've been working with lots and lots of press too. It's been fascinating for me to see Mastroianni, Sophia, all these wonderful actors and great stars comport themselves. Marcello, who has no dialogue, makes every moment count on screen. When Julia Roberts comes on for just a week's work, she behaves in a totally professional fashion, very gifted, and it's surprising. The actors you expect to be tough are easy, the actors you expect to be easy are tough.

S: Bob is famous for creating a great family atmosphere.

L: He creates a world!

S: How is it working with me the first time? he said strangely!

L: Well, it's been thrilling! It's great for me to see not only how professional you are, of course I knew that, and how good you are, which I also knew, and not because I'm your mother, but I can see how people respond to you—it's not me. Like Stephen Rea, who is both of ours favorite fellow in the world—and a great actor—and he adores you. It's so great for me, as your mother, to see those things.

S: Ya, but has it been strange for you?

L: No. I love to see you. I get to see you every day!

S: It's strange for me. I was used to being on your set as your kid. Now I have a different role—I'm here, I'm an actor.

L: And it's always kind of bothered you a bit, you know. How do you feel? Do you have to maintain a certain distance for your own persona?

S: For that, and also character stuff too. I didn't go into this with any expectations, just an open head—a very, very, very open head! OK, which was your favorite fashion show?

L: Issey Miyake. I would like to be that serene.

S: You heard it here first, folks, on FAD-TV!!

L: The first day you wore your wardrobe, you thought, God! I'd never wear any of this...

S: Now I've got to have it all!!

L: Yes, you do, you want it all!

S: But I can see you with a White Sox cap on...

L: Stop—no one is making fun of fashion here. Bob won't. We aren't. Nobody.

Tracey Ullman
The Diary

Tuesday March 1st
Arrived in Paris—
I have caught
tonsillitis from
my children so was
immediately
attended by an
Alain Delon look-
alike doctor who
said "Would you
like maybe, I sink,
to remove your
blouse? It's a
Nicole Farhi vest,
actually Doc, over
a Margaret Howell
lisle cotton
sweater .

Wednesday March 2nd

Penicillin kicking in. Had a costume fitting—Paul Smith has been very generous in lending us his new women's collection. I think Joey Richardson looked longer and leaner in the Vogue feature, but I love that the jackets cover the derriere and don't cut you under the armpits—need a skosh more room in the trews though, Paul. "Paul Smeez," said our French costume lady, "I sink eez très chic, yes?"

Bumped into Sally Kellerman [Harper's Bazaar U.S. editor] and Linda Hunt [U.S. Elle]—"We hear you're really into this?" they say. "We don't give a shit about clothes, whatever's comfortable, you know."

Had an appointment at Chanel to obtain the mandatory suit. Waited ten minutes to be admitted—it's like getting into the U.N. Very friendly, perfectly turned-out French ladies outfitted me in a relaxed marine blue flared-sleeve-and-skirt number—very Liz Tilberis, they pronounced. I attempted Anna Wintour's short-skirt, box-jacket signature look, but I'm not a size 2, and the ladies tutted in that French way, "No, no, Madame. It is not pour vous."

Braved Galeries Lafayette for boots—knee high, square toe, elegant heel—forget it, it's spring. Schlepped around St. Germain, found some medium-priced examples, but how do you put medium-quality boots with a Chanel suit? It's like serviettes at La Gavroche. I was in pain. I returned to base.

Bob gave a welcoming speech to the assembled cast. Marcello Mastroianni claimed that he hadn't read a script yet. Kim Basinger looked jet-lagged. Lyle Lovett grinned impishly as everyone asked, "Where's Julia?" Rupert Everett and Sally Kellerman look like models, so long and willowy. Ute Lemper sat, eight months pregnant, next to Stephen Rea and Forest Whitaker, reunited since The Crying Game. The list goes on...

All actors are the same at the start of a movie—terrified, snatching at information, trying to latch onto an attitude. Sally Kellerman has already bagged the Polly Mellen expression, "Chills, Yves, chills," uttered orgasmically at particularly good shows.

Bob, our leader, introduced everyone and told us that we were about to embark on a gargantuan task under extreme media pressure, that we were dealing with a highly sensitive, war fashion world, afraid to pronounce us good or bad. Who wants to be the first to stick their neck out? Everyone enjoy yourselves, he said, improvise, have a great time, that is what you are here for. What a guy! We are all here because of him—there are no company guys hanging around in Armani suits, being creative with one eye on the budget, trying to make the ending more palatable for Chuck and Nancy in Iowa—thank God.

We left our meeting empowered. Lauren Bacall was being accosted by

*
"
* TRES
BIEN!!

BON!!
→
greaT

a horde of paparazzi as we marched back to our youth hostels (well, this is an Altman film).

Thursday March 3rd

Slept late—no kids.

Ran to Carita for a facial, eyelash curl (a Parisian specialty) and a much-needed manicure and pedicure. After a winter of tramping around in my motorcycle boots, I have about three toenails left...much tutting from the hopeless French beautician.

That afternoon, I had a note from the director, "Be snob who's really from Dagenham," suggests Bob. Ah, yes, back to the class system, my obsession.

A cast party at Le Lark is very interesting. On one side we have Marcello, Sophia, Anouk Aimee, but when the supermodels arrive, the room is electrified. What stars they have become!—and let me tell you, they don't disappoint in the flesh. Claudia, Helen, Kate, Tatiana, have complexions and deportments to die for. A marvelous time is had by all, and I crawl in at 3:30 in the morning, reeking of cigarette smoke and hoarse with laughter from singing past Eurovision contest entries with Helena Christiansen.

Friday March 4th

Threw all my costumes out today and went for what I feel and look good in—Gaultier. As I put in his clothes I become relaxed, confident, and chic—Anna has Chanel, I have Gaultier. He's a real tailor.

Ozbek's show was wonderful, beautiful. Shearling cuffs on coats—Turkish influence throughout—gold-painted feet and rose petals littering the runway. On to Comme des Garçons—very Warsaw ghetto—the girls looked as if they had crippling period pains. Rupert Everett pointed out Linda E. Schindlerlista...très witty. How do you hail a cab when you have no armholes, Rei? Danny Aiello and Stephen Rea looked gobsmacked. Who wants to look like a lollipop, huh? said Danny. Jeez, what a crush. Does everyone smoke in Paris? Yes, chain-like.

Saturday March 5th

The costume department is like an Aladdin's Cave of designer clothes. I walk along the racks and take great armfuls of silk, chain mail, gabardine, and fake fur to my nose, deeply inhaling the chemicals that help the textile industry create 50% of the world's pollution (must remind Vogue to do an article on this—some chance!).

Things are tense. Bob has the flu and lies on his couch covered in a Vivienne Westwood coat, receiving people. The cigarette smoke in our hermetically sealed offices is like a fog. Blinded and gasping, I depart for Paul Smith's show, followed by Montana, then onto to Ann Demeulemeester for women in their 30s who remember the

70s—how your art teacher should dress.

British <u>Vogue</u> took me in their school bus. "Versace was totally over the top, gaudy and vulgar," says one passenger. "So how was it?" queries a willowy blonde. "Oh, brilliant."

Sunday March 6th

D-Day—up at 6:00 A.M. Bob looks fragile but his eyes glint like steel. It's time. I flip my hair on top à la Suzy Menkes or is it Patsy's in <u>Absolutely Fabulous</u>? Out we go, onto the floor. We melt in pretty well. Sophia and Kim blinded by an incredible bank of paparazzi—it gets frightening. We start to talk in character. It feels good. We watch the real McCoy watching us and feel phony, then defensive. This movie was inevitable. It was only a matter of time so we get used to it.

Lacroix's show to me has a South American theme. I'm told later by Elsa Klensch that it was Russian—"A lot of dressing gowns on the runway this year, don't you think Elsa?" "We don't call them dressing gowns, dear," she replies, correcting me again. "Soft-lapeled full-length robes." "Oh, you mean dressing gowns, Elsa?"

Suzy Menkes types out horrified exclamations to her editor—"Hollywood has invaded the runways. Things are chaotic. Stop"—she sees me peeking over her shoulder and snaps her laptop shut.

Rykiel over, we take a break, and Stephen Rea and I gate-crash Westwood's show. Wow, she's come a long way from the SEX shop in the Kings Road. I sit next to Veruschka, who gasps at model Nadja Auerman's legs. She's tall, that girl, says the legendary beauty. Tall? She looks like she's on stilts. We spot film director Mike Figgis filming—rivalry?

On to Gaultier. I'm at fever pitch. This is a dream come true. It's superb. I lose any character I've been cultivating and just gasp and grin from ear to ear. The king, my hero—I tell him this is a character after the show. As I step up to meet him, I start to hyperventilate; pushing Lauren Bacall aside, I tell him that I worship the ground he walks on. I can die now.

Monday March 7th

Work late. Dior this morning which is beautifully presented by Gianfranco Ferré, a man who loves his pasta. In character I tell him I have a house in Tuscany and how we'd love to do a piece on him in the kitchen—does he cook? Lyle Lovett asks him if Mr. Dior is unwell, Gianfranco looks bemused.

Issey Miyake's theme of edible and functional hats in his show appealed to Sam Robards and Lili Taylor in particular (the young liberal un-bodyconscious cast members). Miyake is charming, Stephen Rea accosts The Edge, from U2, whose girlfriend danced so beautifully in the show, and goes on camera with him—very authentic.

Tuesday March 8th

Richard Grant's first day. Richard is dressed by Vivienne Westwood—eight-inch platforms, oversized gangster hat, and white makeup. I have to assist him on the moving staircases in the Louvre as he threatens to topple over—he loves the attention!

Wednesday March 9th

Day off!

Thursday March 10th

Woke up after a very social night with our wonderful cast—four in the morning talks at the Val D'Isère after an irritating party at Le Larc where the lesser beings were cordoned off with the red rope from the "big girls" (as described by Thierry, the owner).

Richard Grant has a ticket for the Chanel show. I don't. As of this entry, Karl the King has decided to abstain from moviemaking so tickets have been thin on the ground. Should I attempt to crash it? I lie in bed wanting to sleep but then I jump up, fling open the windows, and scream, "I'm in Paris, I will probably never get the opportunity again."

I get in! Not only in, but into the inner sanctum—backstage where Karl, fan in hand, is holding forth. I am introduced and immediately plead with him to be in the movie, this social document that he will regret being absent from in twenty years if not sooner. He is very charming and insists that he is not an actor. I suggest that he should just choose his own moment as his presence is sorely missed. Eventually I am led away by one of his courtiers and bump into Jeff Banks from The Clothes Show who gives me his ticket—Karl's concession to the movie is a film can bearing the Chanel Cs on every seat.

The Chanel show is fast and furious, passing in a blur. The girls look a little tired—it's the last big show. New York in two weeks, I hear people say—God, it never ends. We breakfast with Naomi and I talk about the stage school we both attended; Kate and I reminisce about growing up in the Croydon area—always being the girls who had to run for the 10:37 P.M. last train to suburbia. We say we don't miss the net curtains twitching disapprovingly as we came home late nor the ritual cleaning of the Marinas on Sunday morning.

Richard and I wander over to Gaultier's. I love the Parisian shop because you can pick up samples, and I do—in the form of a denim frock coat. It's expensive but I bite the bullet on this one as I'm told that it has been fashioned from Gaultier's own jeans...I am now wearing his groin on my breast—I couldn't be happier.

To be continued...if the readers would like to hear more about the on-set insights into cast squabbles, torrid affairs, strained Anglo-French relations, unexpected nudity etc., etc. On second thoughts, I've had a better offer from a well-known tabloid.

So, à bientôt from Tessy Hoolman (French pronunciation).

the script

INT/EXT

- MOSCOW - GUM DEPARTMENT STORE/CHRISTIAN DIOR SHOP - DAY.

People shopping. SERGEI OBLOMOV, a 60-year-old man, purchases two identical neckties. He leaves the store. CAMERA follows him outside and passes several indigent citizens as we lose him in the enormous expanse of RED SQUARE in MOSCOW.

MAIN TITLES ARE IN RUSSIAN. Crude subtitles appear beneath them in ENGLISH or FRENCH or GERMAN or whatever language is appropriate to the country where the film is being shown. When the CAMERA reaches its widest point, revealing Red Square, we:

WHIP PAN across Europe TO:

EXT - PARIS - DAY

And settle on the Eiffel Tower. Camera tilts down and zooms into the window of a luxurious apartment.

INT/EXT - DE LA FONTAINE MAISON - BEDROOM - DAY

OLIVIER DE LA FONTAINE, head of the Chambre Syndicale, elegantly dressed in a blue suit, is preparing to go out. His Indonesian butler/chauffeur, KETUT, brings the mail to him in his dressing room on a tray. OLIVIER sees the Russian return address, opens the envelope, finds the tie, which we can see he thinks is ugly.

OLIVIER

Moscou... (Moscow) quel horreur... (How horrid.) Posez ça sur le bureau. (Put that on the desk.)

He reads the note as he heads up the staircase to his closet area.

(LETTER)

Dear Mr. de la Fontaine: Blah, blah, blah, blah... Blah, blah, blah, blah, blah.

As OLIVIER approaches the top of the stairs, he hears his wife, ISABELLA, in her bedroom, scolding her dog, ROBIN, for pooping in the house.

ISABELLA

Robin, Robin... Oh, managia. (I told you not to.) Ho detto che non devi farlo. (It's dirty.) C'est sale, c'est pas bien, t'as compris, c'est pas bien, (You shouldn't do that, you understand.) je n'aime pas ça du tout. (Not in the house.)

When OLIVIER reaches the top of the stairs, he finds ISABELLA standing at her door.

ISABELLA

(To OLIVIER)

Stronzo. (You're a shit.)

ISABELLA slams the door in his face. OLIVIER goes to his closet, stepping in the dog poop.

INT - DE LA FONTAINE MAISON - WALK-IN CLOSET - DAY

A closet full of expensive suits. OLIVIER is holding the tie against his many suits, shaking his head, finally pulling a gray suit off a hanger. He takes it into the bedroom where a TV set is on, and we ZOOM in on the beginning of KITTY POTTER's On the Scene.

INT - TV SCREEN - DAY

KITTY begins to explain that this is the beginning of Prêt-à-Porter week in Paris.

KITTY

This is Kitty Potter on the scene for FAD-TV. At the moment, Paris fashion is a thrilling bore. But as of tomorrow, all of that could change. Tomorrow is the first day of the Prêt-à-Porter collection. It's a strange and exhilarating moment for fashion. The only rule is, there are no rules. C'mon with Kitty. We'll be going backstage to sip Diet Coke with all the top models, and we'll meet designers from supernovas to super nobodies. Now let's go behind the scenes and into the busy workrooms of some of fashion's biggest thinkers. Shall we?

CAMERA cuts away from her illustrating what she is telling us. We go to many different designers, real and fictional. Designers at work in their ateliers preparing the clothes, producing the shows, rehearsing the models, and selecting the music. We get a quick explanation of the entire process, illustrated by SHOTS of several REAL DESIGNERS and MODELS. KITTY and her crew are in the busy atelier of THIERRY MUGLER.

KITTY

Can we roll? Uh—This is Kitty Potter in Paris, and I'm here with Thierry Mugler—the cutting edge couturier who's known for his sartorial shock tactics. Thierry, Thierry... it's been said... it's been said that your clothes have a kind of overt, extreme, sexual subtext which is squarely at odds with the image of women as capable and independent of men. I was just wondering—our audience would love to know, really—what you think about that?

THIERRY

Well, it's all about looking good... helping the silhouette...and it's all about getting a great fuck, honey.

KITTY

Oh... well... thank you. Thank you very much. Well, that was designer Thierry Mugler explaining his unique views on style. This is Kitty Potter from Paris, and we're backstage with FAD.

EXT - DOG FASHION SHOW - DAY
A dog fashion show is in progress.

ANNOUNCER
Une touche de légèréte maintenant pour nous rappeler...

Backstage, ISABELLA DE LA FONTAINE brushes her dog's hair. She is competing at an outdoor dog fashion show near Paris. Prefect of Police HENRI TANTPIS is there.

ISABELLA
Comme t'es beau, comme t'es beau. (How beautiful you are.)

TANTPIS
Bonjour, Madame. Le Commissaire Tantpis. J'ai déjà eu le plaisir de vous être presenté, d'ailleurs je vous présente mon chien, Ladd. (I'm Inspector Tantpis. I'd like to introduce my dog, Ladd.)

ISABELLA
Ah, je me souviens de votre chien. (Oh yes, I remember your dog.)

TANTPIS
Au pied. (Heel, Ladd!)

ISABELLA
On va creper ici, voila tu seras beau. (I'm going to pouf your hair. You'll be more beautiful.)

INT - SIMONE LO'S - ATELIER - DAY
The KITTY POTTER TV show continues on a TV set in the atelier. SIMONE LOWENTHAL, a designer, her assistant and chief seamstress PILAR, are working with a couple of models in various stages of undress. Her son, JACK LOWENTHAL, is being interviewed by FIONA ULRICH, a photo journalist from the New York Times. The scene is chaotic. DANE and KIKI, two stunning models, are there.

SIMONE
You move faster, huh? Okay, now you finish. And I'd like to see Kiki and Dane.

PILAR
Okay, thank you.

SIMONE
Okay?

PILAR
Okay.

SIMONE
But quickly, because we are very late.

PILAR
Okay, Kiki. C'mon.

SIMONE
Kiki, can you stop smoking, please.

ALBERTINE enters. She is very pregnant. SIMONE greets her. JACK sees her, becomes a bit nervous, ends his interview and goes to join them.

SIMONE
Oh, who's there? It's wonderful.

ALBERTINE
Yeah, well great things happen to me.

SIMONE
Twins, no?

ALBERTINE
Egg and sperm, and they loved each other. No, triplets.

SIMONE
Wonderful.

JACK
Albertine, you've kept a secret from us. Who's the unlucky man?

ALBERTINE
Well, maybe it's you, darling.

SIMONE
C'mon, Kiki, Dane.

(claps her hands)

Dane. Kiki.

ALBERTINE

I'm sorry, Simone. I won't be able to be in your défilé this year.

SIMONE

Oh, don't worry. No problem.

(to PILAR)

You'll get me Eve, huh?

PILAR

Eve?

OLIVIER arrives wearing a gray suit, and the TIE. He kisses SIMONE.

OLIVIER

Albertine, oh, what have we here?

ALBERTINE

Big fish in the trunk.

OLIVIER

How extraordinary. And, uh, when did this happen?

ALBERTINE

About eight-and-a-half months ago. Exactly.

SIMONE

Mais qu'est ce que c'est que cette cravate divine? (What's with this divine tie?) Tu es devenu daltonien, ou c'est ta femme qui t'en a fait cadeau? (Are you color blind or did your wife give it to you?)

OLIVIER

Non, non, c'est une vielle cravate... (No, no. It's an old one...) Non... non, s'il te plaît, je n'ai pas le temps, il faut que j'y aille. (No, no, please. I'm in a hurry. I've got to go.)

ALBERTINE

(to FIONA)

I am not anymore of any interest to the New York Times, because I just stopped working.

FIONA

I'd love to talk to you.

ALBERTINE

Really?

FIONA

Great.

SIMONE

Ou tu vas? (Where are you going?)

OLIVIER

A Roissy. (To the airport.)

SIMONE

A Roissy, tu as un défilé a Roissy? (There's a fashion show at the airport?)

OLIVIER

Non, je t'en prie, ne dis pas n'importe quoi. (Don't be silly.) J'ai un type qui m'a donné un rendez-vous la bas pour le retrouver. (I'm going to meet someone.) On se voit au dinner? (Will I see you for dinner?)

SIMONE

Je reste ici jusqu'à là répet. (I'll be right here.)

OLIVIER

D'accord.

SIMONE

D'accord.

EXT AIRPORT - INTERNATIONAL ARRIVALS AREA - DAY

KETUT drives OLIVIER's LIMO to the curb. OLIVIER gets out and heads into the terminal.

OLIVIER

Je ne sais pas pour combien de temps j'en ai. (I don't know how long I'll be.)

INT AIRPORT - PASSPORT CONTROL - DAY

SERGEI, our Russian from scene #1, arrives. He wears the same tie as the one OLIVIER received (and is now wearing). He walks through passport control.

INT - AIRPORT - INTERNATIONAL ARRIVALS AREA - DAY

PRÊT à PORTER
de R. ALTMAN
Photo : E. GEORGES
Date : 13/3/94

13

KITTY POTTER and SOPHIE arrive with the rest of the crew.
KITTY
How about right here? This is good.
INT - AIRPORT - CHICAGO CAROUSEL - DAY
The baggage is coming along the carousel. SLIM CHRYSLER, a former Vogue editor, waits
impatiently with CLINT LAMMEREAUX, a boot-wearing Texan who is directing a PORTER to
unload crates marked with the words STINGERS, SIDEWINDERS, COBRAS, SCORPIONS, BLACK
WIDOWS, etc. SLIM is color blind and tries her best to hide it.
SLIM
Yoo hoo—I think this is, yeah, but it's mine.
REGINA KRUMM, an Elle editor, points out her luggage to her assistant, CRAIG GRANT.
REGINA KRUMM
This one coming up is mine. All right, that's one. Now, I don't—I don't think that's
mine.
SISSY WANAMAKER, a U.S. Harper's Bazaar editor, scolds her assistant, Viviene.
SISSY
Do you know what my luggage looks like?
VIVIENE
Yeah. Are you sure it was green?
SISSY
Yes, I'm sure it's green, darling. It's green, it's brown, it's big...
NINA SCANT, a British Vogue editor, chats with SLIM and CLINT.
NINA
Where are you from?
CLINT
Uh—from—uh—Texas.
NINA
I love that accent. I love it. It's so cordial. Would you say—uh—"Thank you, ma'am"?
Would you just say that for me once.
CLINT
Well, maybe later.
MILO O'BRANAGAN, a superstar photographer, is with his entourage, WINNIE and ALAIN, who
are fretting over his camera cases and luggage.
MILO
He knows the Polaroids are not supposed to travel in the box. I could be in the hotel by
now.
Behind them, standing at the baggage conveyor belt in somewhat of a daze, is ANNE
EISENHOWER, Houston Chronicle reporter. She wears a wine-stained T shirt with WORLD'S
GREATEST MOM printed on it. She got drunk on the flight and is now a little hungover. All
she carries with her is her laptop computer. ANNE bumps into LOUISE HAMILTON, a tourist
passenger, who picks up her two battered Samsonite bags from the belt.
LOUISE
Oh.
ANNE
I'm so sorry.
LOUISE
Excuse me.
ANNE
So sorry.
LOUISE
That's okay, okay. Are you all right?
ANNE
I lost my suitcase.
LOUISE
Oh. Well, you just report it over there to lost luggage.
ANNE
Oh, well, it's not, it's not that. I left it in the airport bar in Houston, that's where
I came in from. I'm kinda scared to fly, so I went in there to get my courage, if you
know what I mean.
SISSY and NINA argue over the luggage.

SISSY
Would you read the tag?
NINA
Sissy, I'm sorry. This is yours.
VIVIENE
Hey! Don't kick...
SISSY
Viviene!
VIVIENE
Qu'est-ce que tu fais. (What are you doing?)
LOUISE tries to get away from ANNE.
LOUISE
You know, they'll find it. That's what they're very good at. All you do is just tell them.
ANNE
It's nice of you to say that. It's nice of you to care. But, you see, I don't speak French. That's the thing. Well, high school. But, you know, that doesn't really count. And I don't even know the French word for baggage.
LOUISE
It's bagage. Just like baggage, bagage.
SOPHIE spots OLIVIER and points him out to KITTY and forces him into an interview.
KITTY
You got the cards ready? You ready? We need a longer cord on this thing.
SOPHIE
Vous pouvez répondre à deux ou trois questions pour Kitty Potter?
OLIVIER
Vraiment très vite, parce que je suis très pressé.
Sophie whispers to Kitty who Olivier is.
KITTY
Hello, Olivier.
OLIVIER
Hi, Kitty.
KITTY
Oh, what a pretty tie? And it's got kitties on it. And I'm Kitty. Let me guess. Charvet or Dior.
OLIVIER
C'est Dior, naturellement.
KITTY
Oh! Bingo!
SERGEI walks past a custodian's cart, looks both ways and tosses his passport in the trash can. He replaces his Russian hat with a French cap.
KITTY begins her interview with OLIVIER.
KITTY
This is Kitty Potter at Charles de Gaulle airport, where what I like to call the "international intelligentsia of fashion in all its many mutations," is arriving all around me. Are we expecting someone special here today?
OLIVIER
Special?
KITTY
Um—uh, well, le tout Paree has been buzzin' about a lollopolooza called Liza, and her definite, maybe, appearance on the runway at Chanel. And I know that she is due any minute... Any possibility that you might be here for her?
OLIVIER
Well, I'm here to welcome the press and the retailers. I'm here to welcome you, Kitty. Welcome. I think it's going to be a great season.
KITTY
Well, we all know how Liza just loves the spotlight, so I was just wondering if you could give us a little—just shed some light on that subject for us. Olivier?
SERGEI spies OLIVIER being interviewed, walks past him, and adjusts his tie, thus getting OLIVIER's attention.

KITTY
Olivier? Sir?
OLIVIER
Um—our new facilities are sublime. It's a giant step forward for Paris fashion. The designers are thrilled.
KITTY
Well, I bet they are. Um, uh—
OLIVIER
Will you excuse me?
KITTY
Cou-cou-cou-could-uh. Well, there he goes with the absolute poise of an architect's desk lamp.
OLIVIER walks after SERGEI to a snack counter. LOUISE passes by with her cart; she can't lose ANNE.
ANNE
Are you here for the Prêt-à-Porter? I'm with the Houston Chronicle. I'm the assistant fashion editor. My boss was supposed to come, but she got sick with the flu.
OLIVIER and SERGEI wait at the airport snack counter.
OLIVIER
Je n'ai pas eu le temps de prendre mon petit déjeuner ce matin. (I didn't have time for breakfast.) Ce la va tres mal avec cette cravate. Il faut que je me change. (I had to change my shirt to wear this ridiculous tie.) Un sandwich, s'il vous plaît. (A sandwich, please.)
KITTY interviews REGINA, NINA, and SISSY.
KITTY
And here we have the Paris troika! The three Powers That Be in the world of magazine editing. The unflinchingly fabulous Sissy Wanamaker of Harper's Bazaar. Hi, Sissy.
SISSY
Hello, Kitty. Hello.
KITTY
The unstoppably sophisticated Nina Scant from British Vogue.
NINA
Lord, I've never heard myself described like that before. Hello.
KITTY
And the relentlessly artistic Regina Krumm from Elle. Hey...
REGINA
Hey.
KITTY
Welcome to Paris, girls.
OLIVIER is handed a sandwich by the snack shop WAITRESS.
WAITRESS
Merci.
OLIVIER
Merci.
SERGEI
Il est a quoi? (What kind is it?)
OLIVIER
Au jambon. (Ham.)
SERGEI
Le jambon a Moscou, niet. (There's no ham in Moscow.)
We return to Kitty's interview.
NINA
They're very diverting—both magazines—but I still think Vogue is the final word, Kitty. I think you'll have to agree with me there. I have to go!
REGINA and SISSY try to get a word in.
OLIVIER turns away from the counter.
OLIVIER
Allons dans ma voiture. Vous marchez derriere moi, s'il vous plaît. (Follow me to my car, please.)
MAJOR HAMILTON, a buyer for Marshall Field's, has come through the customs area and has

been listening to the interview. He wears a bow tie and is pompous and overbearing, ordering people around.
MAJOR
Kitty, Kitty Potter! I don't suppose you'd remember me: Major Hamilton. Marshall Field's. Chicago. Fashion Director. It's good seeing you. I had a little bit of time. Would you like a quick interview?
KITTY
We really don't do unscheduled interviews.
MAJOR
Oh, I don't mind. I don't mind at all. Are you sure?
MILO has come through the customs area with his entourage. SOPHIE runs up to him.
KITTY
Milo, Milo. One minute, one minute... Hey, how are you? Kitty Potter, Kitty Potter.
MAJOR
I'll be here if you need me.
KITTY
Are we ready? We rolling? This is Milo O'Branagan, the most sought-after fashion photographer in the business today. Milo, you've had a lock on the look of the 90s for decades now. How have you managed to stay on top of everything?
MILO
Probably the same way you have, Kitty.
KITTY
Just hard work and believing in yourself, right?
MILO
Taking advantage of other people's insecurities.
INT - SIMONE LO'S ATELIER - DAY
SIMONE and PENELOPE descend the stairs.
SIMONE
Anyway, we'll show it to Pilar.
JACK is still being interviewed by FIONA.
FIONA
So, does your mother believe in the old adage that some women dress for men, but most women dress for other women?
JACK
You know, my mother makes dresses for herself. Dressing for men has never particularly interested her, although she's certainly undressed for a few of them. You know the main difference between men and women in fashion is this: women make dresses for themselves and for other women... a man makes clothes for the woman he wants to be with, or in most cases, the woman he wants to be.
FIONA
Are you married?
JACK
Mmm-hmm. I'm married to Dane. Come over here, honey.
KIKI rises from her chair and walks to Jack. DANE remains seated, talking on the telephone.
JACK
Dane, yoo-hoo. Earth to Dane.
DANE
Try and be a little bit nice.
JACK
This is my wife, Dane. These are her famous legs, and this is her famous sister, Kiki.
KIKI
(to FIONA)
Hey, how's it going?
FIONA
Hello. Fiona.
DANE
Hey, Fiona, how do you do? Charmed.
JACK
They share the same father, or at least that's what their agent tells us.

INT - CY BIANCO'S ATELIER - DAY
CY BIANCO, his assistant, REGGIE and a few other ASSISTANTS are working with some MODELS.
ALBERTINE, the pregnant model, is being yelled at by CY.
CY
I made these clothes for your old body and now you couldn't fit into them if I asked you
to. Am I crazy? Am I crazy or what?
REGGIE
Cy, it wasn't her fault.
ALBERTINE
It wasn't my fault. It wasn't my fault, you faggot, you woman-hater. It was great, a big
shock.
CY
You could have called me, right? You could have called.
ALBERTINE
I was in Germany.
CY
Oh, I am crazy, I am crazy. Or did the the goddamn Germans invent the telephone?
ALBERTINE
They invented worse, okay? I wasn't sure I was going to keep it.
CY
Look, you gotta be eight-and-a-half months pregnant. I mean, if I was Lacroix... if I was
that thief Lagerfeld, you would've called me, right?
REGGIE
We'll get Eve. They are the same size.
CY
I hate her fucking tattooed head.
INT - CORT ROMNEY'S ATELIER - DAY
CORT ROMNEY, his wife, VIOLETTA, and several ASSISTANTS are working with a model. The
atmosphere is quite different from CY'S. Very calm, serene. CORT ROMNEY is studying a
garment on a model named EVE. She has shorn hair and a tattoo on her scalp.
CORT ROMNEY
You're bald. Violetta, I can't deal with this girl.
VIOLETTA
Well, I'll get rid of her.
CORT ROMNEY
Albertine. Albertine's the one I want. Why can't I have Albertine?
VIOLETTA
Albertine is pregnant. The agency said she was pregnant.
CORT ROMNEY
Pregnant is not my silhouette this season. I mean, it is not, it is not, it is not. My
bulge is in the bustle out of the back... not in the belly up front. Bald tattoo is not
part of my vision. It's beyond déjà vu.
EXT - PARIS - PAN TO PONT ALEXANDRE III - DAY
A traffic jam on the Pont Alexandre III. FIONA is there taking pictures. The traffic
builds up.
EXT - PONT ALEXANDRE III - TRAFFIC JAM - DAY
OLIVIER's car is in the center of the traffic jam. Horns are honking. People are
beginning to get out of their cars to see what the problem is. OLIVIER and SERGEI are
having an animated conversation. OLIVIER eats his ham sandwich.
OLIVIER
(to KETUT)
Dites moi, allez voir ce qui se passe. C'est insupportable. (Go see what's wrong with
this traffic.)
KETUT jumps out of the limo to check what's going on.
SERGEI
Oui, bien sûr, je ne voudrais pas parler de ma femme. (We have to talk about your wife.)
OLIVIER
Enfin, bon, écoutez, encore une fois cela me fait plaisir de vous voir mais je suis
quandmême un petit peu etonné de vous voir arriver comme ça. (I don't understand what my
wife has to do with you.)

ÊT à PORTER
R. ALTMAN
oto : E. GEORGES
te :
17/3/94

12

Suddenly, OLIVIER chokes on a piece of ham fat. He can't get his breath. SERGEI beats him on the back but can't dislodge the obstruction.
SERGEI
(In Italian)
You shouldn't eat so fast!
OLIVIER gasps and dies. SERGEI is in a bad spot. He gets out of the car and tries to sneak away. KETUT returns to the car and sees SERGEI leaving hurriedly. KETUT looks into the backseat and sees OLIVIER slumped over. He shakes him in an attempt to revive him.
KETUT
Monsieur, Monsieur!
He realizes his employer is dead. SERGEI begins to run. He jumps on the trunk of a stuck car and starts running over car hoods and roofs. KETUT yells out to a policeman.
KETUT
Arretez le, arretez le! Assassin! Assassin!(Stop that man! He's a murderer!)
EXT - PONT ALEXANDRE III - TRAFFIC JAM - DAY
A traffic POLICEMAN starts to chase SERGEI. FIONA aims her camera, with its very long lens, at the escaping SERGEI. She expertly clicks off several exposures.
EXT - PONT ALEXANDRE III - BRIDGE - DAY
SERGEI dives into the Seine. Some of the people stuck in the traffic jam are out of their vehicles watching.
EXT - PONT ALEXANDRE III - THE SEINE - DAY
Rings of the wake mark the the spot where SERGEI went in. We don't see him surface.
INT - SIMONE LO'S ATELIER - DAY
SIMONE is working. JACK, KIKI, DANE, PILAR and ALBERTINE are all still there.
SIMONE
Pilar, the two grays is not good, you know. Pilar...
PILAR
(into telephone)
What? Are you joking? Hold on, please. Simone...
SIMONE
Why there is no music today here?
PILAR
S'il vous plaît, Simone, it's important.
SIMONE
Okay, I'm coming. Oh, your smoke, Pilar. You are killing us.
She finally gets to the phone.
SIMONE
(into phone)
Oui? Oui, c'est moi. Murdered?
PILAR
Jack!
SIMONE
(to office)
Put on the news.
(into phone)
C'est pas possible. He was here.
On TV, a French news report gives the first sketchy details of OLIVIER's death. SIMONE turns to the others.
SIMONE
Olivier's been murdered...
(into phone)
Does his wife know that?
EXT - DOG SHOW - DAY
Two POLICE OFFICERS arrive; one whispers to TANTPIS. TANTPIS looks for ISABELLA.
TANTPIS
Je vous prie d'accepter mes condoléances. Votre mari est décédé. (Madam, please accept my condolences. Your husband has died.)
ISABELLA
Ah, mais quel dommage. (Oh, what a pity.)
(to her dog)

Viens, ton père est mort. (Your papa has died.)

TANTPIS
Excusez... de vous interrompre... Mon metier est parfois difficile et je suis obligé. (My job is somewhat difficult...) Mais je tiens a vous faire remarquer que j'ai fait mon devoir en vous apprenant cette sinistre nouvelle. (It was my duty to bring you this terrible news.)

ISABELLA
Non, mais mon chien et moi nous sommes très heureux qu'il est mort. (But my dog and I are very happy. We hated him.)

EXT - PONT ALEXANDRE III - BRIDGE AFTER JUMP - DAY

POLICE OFFICERS are already on the scene trying to sort out the traffic jam. TV NEWS CREWS have arrived and are interviewing.

SKY TV REPORTER
We are coming to you live from the historic Pont Alexandre in Paris, where Olivier de la Fontaine...

During the above, POLICE OFFICER questions FIONA. INSPECTOR DANIEL FORGET, a homicide policeman, arrives on the scene. He examines the body of OLIVIER as it is carted away. He notices the TIE. He steps in dog shit on his way to FIONA.

FIONA
(still speaking to POLICEMAN)
Je vois... (I saw...)

FORGET
(also to POLICEMAN)
C'est elle la fille qui a fait les photos? (Is that the girl who took the pictures?)

FIONA
Oui.

FORGET
You took the photographs?

FIONA
Oui.

FORGET
Can I have the roll?

FIONA
Yes. Je veux un reçu. (I want a receipt.)

FORGET
Vous prenez son nom. (Take her name.) You'll give your name.

A NEWSCASTER is interviewing MODELS and a PHOTOGRAPHER whose photo session on the bridge was interrupted by the chaos.

HELENA
...and he just jumped off the bridge, just like that. He just jumped off.

TATIANA
Yeah, well, no, it was totally bizarre. Completely strange.

PHOTOGRAPHER
I saw the whole thing...

Meanwhile, INSPECTOR FORGET questions KETUT.

FORGET
Bon, il est où le chauffeur? (Can you identify the guy.)

KETUT
All white people look alike to me.

FORGET
All right, how could you tell him apart from your boss?

KETUT
By his clothes, how do you think? That's how I tell everybody apart.

EXT - GRAND HOTEL - DAY
Establishing shot.

INT - GRAND HOTEL - LOBBY - DAY

SERGEI stands in the background in a blue janitor's smock. JOE FLYNN, a sports reporter for the Washington Post, is checking out of his room. He plops his bags in the middle of the lobby. His laptop computer is slung over his shoulder. The rest of the cast, except LOUISE, begin to pour into the lobby, fighting for their rooms. ANNE tries to check in,

131

explaining that she left her baggage in Houston and has nothing to wear. She has had a
little too much to drink on the airplane, and we will find later that just one drink
alters her behavior dramatically. VIVIENE is with SISSY. KITTY, SOPHIE and the FAD CREW
set up for interviews in the lobby.

KITTY
(leading her CREW)
C'mon. C'mon. Right around here. Right here.

JOE is at the front desk.

JOE
I'm checking out. Joe Flynn.

SERGEI moves to JOE'S luggage. He looks around the lobby, cautiously, then takes the
bags. SOPHIE snares SLIM for a interview while CLINT chats with a group of models.

SOPHIE
Pardonnez-moi, Madame Chrysler, but that's Kitty Potter over there, from FAD-TV, and...

SLIM
Oui, oui, oui, oui. J'avais promis a l'aeroport. Je vais donner une interview. Oui,
absolument. (I know I promised at the airport that I'm going to give you an interview.
Absolutely.)

KITTY
Slim, Slim, hey, you are so...

SLIM
Hello, Kitty.

At this point ASSISTANTS are bumping into assistants and everyone is trying to check in.
JOE is still at the front desk checking out and ANNE in line behind him waiting to check
in.

MAJOR
What? Am I invisible? I've been standing here for half an hour...

SISSY
I mean, we had to hear you at the airport, I think that's really enough

MAJOR
I'll accept an apology.

RECEPTIONIST
(to JOE)
There's a call for you from Washington. You can use the phone on the desk right there.

JOE goes over to the telephone.

JOE
Hello.

ANNE moves up to the desk to check in.

ANNE
Hi. I'm Anne Eisenhower from the Houston Chronicle. I should have a reservation.

Meanwhile, the Kitty/Slim interview continues.

KITTY
...And the only person, still living, who can give Saint Laurent color tips! Slim, we've
missed you so very much since you, uh, "retired" from Vogue.

SLIM
Really...?

We go back to JOE on the telephone.

JOE
I'm a sports reporter, for Christ's sake. I don't know dick about fashion.

CITY DESK VOICE (over phone)
You're all we've got there, pal. Matthews wants this—

JOE
Oh, for God's sake, I gotta leave Paris. You gotta use a fuckin' wire.

CITY DESK VOICE (over phone)
No can do. This is... is a big story.

JOE
What's so special about this... dead guy? What's his name?

CITY DESK VOICE (over phone)
Who?

JOE

The dead guy!
CITY DESK VOICE (over phone)
De la Fontaine. Olivier de la Fontaine. Got that?
JOE
Yeah, right. And do me a favor, call my wife. She's not gonna believe me.
(slams the phone down)
Fucking cocksucker!
JOE hurries back to the front desk to get his room back. The HOTEL CLERK has just given ANNE the two card keys to Joe's old room. JOE interrupts.
JOE
Whoa, whoa, new ball game. I-I-I-I'm not checking out. I'm not checking out. No, I'm not checking out. I'm not leaving. I'm staying. This is my room. I'm staying.
He grabs one of the card keys from ANNE. She clutches the other one.
ANNE
This is my room!
HOTEL CLERK
Monsieur. Madame.
JOE
Well, you'll find the lady another room. I'm sorry.
HOTEL CLERK
I'm afraid there is no other room, sir.
JOE
Well, that's not my problem. I'm sorry.
ANNE
Excuse me, you clearly don't understand. This is my room. You don't understand the day I've had.
JOE
You don't understand. I haven't checked out.
(rips his credit card bill)
See, I have not checked out.
KITTY and SLIM continue their interview.
KITTY
Well, do we have any fashion plans or projects in the wings anywhere?
SLIM
Well, I think you'll find out about them when the time is right, but now I want you to meet somebody very, very special, of extraordinary talent. Clint! Clint! Come over here. Over here! Clint Lammoreaux meet Kitty Potter.
The chaos continues. JOE still has a key and won't give it up. ANNE has a key and won't give it up. The CLERK gives up. They're all yelling at the same time.
JOE
(to ANNE)
I don't care about your luggage!
ANNE
This is my room.
JOE
You'll have to find the lady another room.
Anne makes a sudden dash for the elevator.
JOE
Hey!
He goes for his baggage and sees it's gone.
JOE
Where's my bag? Where's my bag?
(to a porter)
If you don't find my bag soon, you're gonna hear from the Washington Post. 2326.
(to ANNE)
Hey! Hey!
He rushes after ANNE to catch the elevator. Both run through the KITTY/SLIM interview.
SLIM
Yes, yes, specially that... cotton, pharmaceuticals... you name it...
CLINT

D1014

MIRAMAX FILMS

PRET-A-PORTER
PHOTO: E.GEORGES

D1006

MIRAMAX FILMS

PRET-A-PORTER
PHOTO: E.GEORGES

...cobras, pythons, rattlesnakes... ring lizards...

INT - GRAND HOTEL - HALLWAY

JOE and ANNE race for the room. He tries the card key in a door as ANNE runs up from behind. He pretends to fumble and drop the card key.

JOE

Oh shit!

ANNE

Ha... ha.

JOE rushes across the hall to the correct door. He gets in; ANNE forces her way inside.

ANNE

Hey! Hey! What are you doing? Let me in! Ow! Ow!

INT - GRAND HOTEL - JOE & ANNE'S ROOM - DAY

The room is just the way JOE left it: a total and utter mess. The bed isn't made, towels are on the floor, the TV has been left on, breakfast, partially eaten, is still on the room service cart. JOE and ANNE each run for one of the phone extensions.

JOE

I'm on this line.

She slams down the receiver and opens her laptop computer on the bed.

JOE

Yes, this is Joe Flynn. Now, listen to me if you want to keep your job. Ecoutez... Je veux mon bagage (Listen... I you my baggage) et je vous cette bitch dans ma chambre maintenant. (and I you this bitch in my room, now!) What do you mean you don't have any bagage? I know goddamn well you have my bagage. You think you can smoke me out of here with that cock and bull story? You're as full of shit as a Christmas goose. As full of merde... as a canard...

He sees a news report about OLIVIER on the news. He slams down the receiver. ANNE picks up the phone.

ANNE

Yes, hello this is Anne Eisenhower, as in General Dwight D. Eisenhower. Yes, that's correct, ex-President Dwight D. Eisenhower. No, I know he's not registered here, I am. No, I don't want the manager again. I've talked to the manager. I want... the owner!

JOE

I think this hotel's owned by Sony or some Japanese company. I wonder what time it is in Tokyo?

ANNE

I wonder how long it will take them to get you out of my room, Mr. Joe Flynn.

EXT - HOTEL SPLENDID - DAY

Establishing shot. LOUISE is outside trying to bring in her unwieldy bags when a PORTER comes over to assist her.

LOUISE

(to PORTER)

Oh, thank you. Could you help me with these bags? I'll be checking in here. Ooops, sorry.

INT - HOTEL SPLENDID - LOBBY - DAY

A small TV behind the desk shows a report about people arriving for the Prêt-à-Porter shows. LOUISE checks into the hotel.

LOUISE

Excusez-moi. Oh, sorry. I believe you have a reservation for a Louise Marshall?

RECEPTIONIST

Uh... Marshall?

LOUISE

Uh... Field. Louise Field.

LOUISE catches a glimpse of MAJOR at the airport on the TV.

LOUISE

Huh. Major! Oh! Good-looking guy, huh?

INT - LOUVRE - DAY

KITTY interviews ELSA KLENSCH.

KITTY

Well, bonjour, and I'm standing here with the one, the only, Elsa Klensch.

ELSA KLENSCH

Thank you, Kitty, how are you?

KITTY
How are you doing?
ELSA KLENSCH
I'm fine, darling..
KITTY
Thank you so much for doing this. What's going on in fashion for the 90s?
ELSA KLENSCH
A lot's going on in fashion for the 90s. You know, news is always happening, don't you agree?
KITTY
Well, yes I do. And we depend on you to bring us the news. So, what's going on?
ELSA KLENSCH
Well, this is the most important time, the most important week in fashion. This is where everything happens, really, for the year.
KITTY
Let me ask you this: Did you get any good scoops this morning?
ELSA KLENSCH
Yes... but... ahh...
KITTY
Oh, she's saving it for her own show, folks!
INT - GRAND HOTEL - MAJOR'S ROOM - DAY
MAJOR unpacks and settles in. He finds a pair of women's panties in his suitcase. This distresses him greatly.
MAJOR
What the hell is this!
(picks up the phone)
Operator? Splendid Hotel, please.
INT - SMALLER HOTEL - LOUISE'S ROOM - DAY
LOUISE opens her two nearly empty suitcases. TV continues. She is singing to herself as she unpacks. The phone rings and she answers it. (INTERCUT WITH SCENE ABOVE).
LOUISE
(singing)
Let's begin again...
The phone rings and she stumbles over furniture and suitcases to pick it up.
LOUISE
Aaaah! Hello? Yes?
MAJOR
Goddamnit, Louise. You left a pair of skivvies in my suitcase. You got to be careful about that stuff.
LOUISE
I don't know how it happened. I'm very sorry, and I won't let that happen again, I'll be much more careful... I... ahh... whew... I'm sorry.
MAJOR
And, listen, since when are you so talkative? You were talking to everybody at that airport.
LOUISE
I didn't talk to anyone.
MAJOR
You even started to talk to me! You would have blown our cover.
LOUISE
No, I didn't. Not at all.
MAJOR
You woulda blown our cover. We gotta be careful, honey. Very, very careful. You understand?
LOUISE
I'm very sorry. I'm very sorry, I will be more careful. OK? My darling, do you miss me?
MAJOR
Does a bear shit in the woods?
LOUISE starts laughing uncontrollably. She can't stop herself. She sits on the bed and drops the phone in her lap as her hysterics continue.

INT - LOUVRE - DAY
KITTY continues her interview with ELSA KLENSCH.
KITTY
How was Milan?
ELSA KLENSCH
Well, I'll tell you, I got the surprise of my life there. You know, I know a lot about fashion and we all know that short skirts are back, and short skirts are going to be back for the rest of the 90s—that's my bet... Well, I saw pleated skirts, I saw A-line skirts, I saw sarong skirts, but then suddenly, the poof skirt emerged. Now, you must remember Lacroix's poof skirt? We were poofed and poofed and poofed? Well it could be that we're gonna be poofed again before the turn of the century.
KITTY
Will you be poofed?
ELSA KLENSCH
I doubt it.
INT - GRAND HOTEL - NINA'S SUITE - DAY
A large elegant room filled with gifts and flowers from all the designers. NINA and JEAN-PIERRE, her assistant, arrive with the PORTERS who carry all the luggage.
NINA
Arrête!
JEAN-PIERRE
Arrête! Stop! Stop!
NINA walks to the window.
INT - REGINA'S SUITE - SAME MOMENT
REGINA's suite is practically a carbon copy of NINA's. She enters the same way: with her assistant, CRAIG, and PORTERS carrying all the luggage.
REGINA
Just let me take a look. Stop!
CRAIG
Arrête, s'il vous plaît.
REGINA walks to the window.
INT - NINA'S SUITE - SAME MOMENT
NINA
What suite is Regina Krumm in?
JEAN-PIERRE
Regina? Uh—Foest Street.
NINA
Foest?
JEAN-PIERRE
Yes, Foest Street.
NINA
You mean, Faust.
JEAN-PIERRE
Faust!
NINA
The Faust Suite!
JEAN-PIERRE
Yes, Faust Street.
NINA
That's supposed to be my suite.
INT - REGINA'S SUITE - SAME MOMENT
REGINA
That's the suite that I'm supposed to be in.
CRAIG
Well, this is your suite.
REGINA
No—no. This is not my suite. This is the Faust Suite, I'm supposed to be in the Salomé Suite.
INT - NINA'S SUITE - SAME MOMENT
NINA

I'm not in the Salomé Suite. You get on the phone right now—get on the phone—and tell them that I want to be in the Faust Suite. It's the one I asked for, I don't want to be in the Salomé Suite.

INT - REGINA'S SUITE - SAME MOMENT

REGINA

This is the wrong suite.

CRAIG

This is the wrong suite.

REGINA

I'm supposed to be in the Salomé Suite.

CRAIG

You're supposed to be in the Salomé Suite.

REGINA

(to PORTERS)

And you just—uh—set those things down. Down, down. Yes, 'cause we're going to be moving... I can't believe they would do that to me.

INT - NINA'S SUITE - SAME MOMENT

NINA

Put everything down. Just put it down, because this is not my suite.

INT - GRAND HOTEL - MISC. ROOM #1 - NIGHT

A MAID is cleaning the bathroom. SERGEI, carrying Joe's suitcase, slips into the room and hides. The MAID leaves.

INT - GRAND HOTEL - HALLWAY - DAY

REGINA and NINA step out of their rooms. Behind them, the PORTERS and ASSISTANTS change rooms with all the luggage.

NINA

Regina.

REGINA

Nina.

NINA

Oh my God, here we are again.

REGINA

Here we are again.

NINA

Hmmm...

REGINA

It's unbelievable. It seems like just a second ago.

REGINA

I too. I feel like I have déjà vu.

NINA

Can you believe the construction in this city?

REGINA ·

No. It's wild.

NINA

What are they doing?

REGINA

Well, it must be an awful lot of maintenance.

NINA

Oh my God...

CRAIG and JEAN-PIERRE exchange keys and change rooms.

NINA

...you know, it just goes right up my nostrils.

REGINA

Yes.

NINA

It's incredible.

REGINA

It's horrid. Isn't it.

NINA

Now are you going to the embassy tonight?

REGINA
Oh, of course.
NINA
Well, my darling, I shall see you there. Get some rest.
REGINA
Bye darling.
INT - POLICE DEPARTMENT - DAY
TANTPIS bursts into the room with his wet bull dog, LADD.
TANTPIS
Bon jour.
He passes POLICEMEN who are busy at their desks. He walks past INSPECTOR FORGET who is examining Fiona's photographs of SERGEI escaping. In none of the photos do we ever see SERGEI's face—only what he was wearing. KETUT is there.
TANTPIS
Forget!
INSPECTOR FORGET and KETUT follow TANTPIS to his desk.
TANTPIS
(to POLICE OFFICER)
Bonjour.
TANTPIS sits and looks at the photos.
TANTPIS
Voyons voir cela. Qui est-ce? (Let's see. Who's this?)
FORGET
Chauffeur.
TANTPIS
Qu'est-ce que ça veut dire. On n'y a aucun visage. (What does that mean? We can't see any face.)
TANTPIS flips though the pictures. FORGET shrugs.
KETUT
That's him. That's the man. See? That's his coat. His pants.
FORGET
We know what he wore, but we don't know who he is.
INT - GRAND HOTEL - MISC. ROOM #1 - NIGHT
SERGEI opens JOE's suitcase and pulls out a checkered sport jacket. He tries it on. It's much too long.
INT - GRAND HOTEL - JOE & ANNE'S ROOM - DAY
Joe watches a SKY TV news report of OLIVIER's death. He takes notes.
SKY TV REPORTER
We are coming to you live from the historic Pont Alexandre in Paris where Olivier de la Fontaine, head of the la Chambre de Syndicale de la Mode de la Haute Couture, which is French fashion's governing body, has been murdered in the back of his limousine. Eyewitnesses report that a stocky man possibly mid-sixties exited the car that was stuck in traffic, fleeing the scene by plunging headlong into the Seine. He's believed drowned. If not, he has surely died of pollution. This is a shocking prelude to the Prêt-à-Porter collection, the glittering spectacle Olivier de la Fontaine choreographed each season for a cast of thousands. This is Sandra de la Notte for Sky News.
ANNE comes out of the bathroom and sits on the sofa. JOE glances at her.
JOE
You still here?
INT - CORT ROMNEY'S ATELIER - DAY
The TV continues. FIONA discusses a designer group photo with CORT ROMNEY and his wife, VIOLETTA.
FIONA
It's gonna be a group designer photo. Most everybody's going to be there.
CORT ROMNEY
All the designers are going to be there?
FIONA
Pretty much everybody. I've got Cerruti, Rykiel, Westwood, Montana, Agnes B.
CORT ROMNEY
You don't know these people.

FIONA
Well, they said they're going to be there. Um—Simone Lo will—will probably not be there.
She may not even show her collection.
CORT ROMNEY
Are you serious? Simone is a greedy bitch.
VIOLETTA
Cort—
CORT ROMNEY
Her tears dry before they hit her cheeks.
VIOLETTA
Don't say such things.
CORT ROMNEY
It's true. Simone Lo's collection is little more than crematorium couture. Dead. How
'bout Gaultier?
FIONA
Yeah. He's very enthusiastic.
CORT ROMNEY
Mmmmmmmm...
VIOLETTA
You like his work.
CORT ROMNEY
I used to. The beginning of his career when he was my little protégé. Lately, he's gone
off in a direction I don't think I can entirely approve of.
FIONA
You mean like Cy Bianco?
CORT ROMNEY
Why would you want to dredge up his recycled name?
FIONA
It seems that they're both influenced by the street.
CORT ROMNEY
What street? Bond? Or Camden Lock?
INT - SIMONE'S ATELIER - DAY
DANE is getting into her street clothes.
JACK
Where's mother?
DANE
Um—I think she's in her office.
JACK goes into SIMONE's office.
INT - SIMONE'S OFFICE
JACK enters.
SIMONE
Don't say anything, Jack. Just get out and close the door.
JACK leaves. SIMONE takes off her scarf and gives it to PILAR.
SIMONE
I don't want that black thing.
INT - SIMONE'S ATELIER
JACK approaches his wife, DANE, who is getting dressed.
JACK
I don't think I'm going to be home tonight, honey. My mother wants me to stay with her.
DANE
I wonder who's the father?
JACK
The father?
DANE
You know, Albertine's baby.
JACK
Well, it's not me.
DANE
Oh, really?
JACK

Mm-hm.

JACK turns to go. KIKI follows.

KIKI

Dane, I'm going to try to catch a ride with your old man. I'll catch you later, all right?

DANE

That's nice of him.

INT - CY BIANCO'S ATELIER - DAY

FIONA pitches her designer photo shoot to CY. REGGIE listens in.

FIONA

There's no down side. Um—Milo O'Branagan's the photographer. You can't do better than that. He's the best. He will make you all look great.

CY BIANCO

Milo O'Branagan?

FIONA

And you'll be, what, with your friends.

CY BIANCO

(to MODEL)

Oooooh, that's nice.

FIONA

He shoots quick.

CY BIANCO

(re: model's outfit)

This is nice. Is it wrong? No, it's definitely not wrong. Milo, huh?

FIONA

Yeah. Milo. He's the best.

CY BIANCO

How'd you get him? You sleep with him or what?

FIONA

No, I don't sleep with men.

INT - GRAND HOTEL - CLINT'S SUITE - DAY

The mysterious trunks are opened to reveal cowboy boots. CLINT carefully examines the crates' contents. JACK enters with EVE, the model from ROMNEY's atelier.

JACK

Where is Mr. Lammereaux?

SLIM

Jack, wait till you see these boots. One for every mood.

JACK

Elles sont hallucinantes. Elles sont craquantes. (How cool.) Clint, how are you? It's been such a long time since Christmas. How is Anne? She is absolutely charming. Do you know Anne Richards?

SLIM

I introduced you to her. Remember me?

JACK

Ev, Clint Lammereaux. Ev, Slim Chrysler.

(to SLIM)

C'est incroyable. Ecoute... <u>Women's Wear Daily</u> va adorer ça... Simone aussi. (It's unbelievable. Listen... <u>Women's Wear Daily</u> is going to adore it... and Simone too.)

SLIM

Je ne suis pas sûr de ça. Parce que Simone elle a son propre goût. (I'm not so sure about that. Simone has her own taste.)

JACK

Oh, t'es pessismiste. (You're pessimistic.)

SLIM

Oui, c'est ga. (She does.)

CLINT

How's that?

JACK

Well, Slim was just saying that my mother is really going to love these boots. She's going to love them.

INT - GRAND HOTEL - MILO'S ROOM - NIGHT
Milo meets with Regina. Her assistant, Craig, stands behind her. Milo's entourage is everywhere.
MILO
Well, nice of you to say so, but—uh—I'm just a simple Irish country boy who loves his work.
REGINA
Uh—listen. I know your contract with Vogue is almost up.
The doorbell rings.
CRAIG
March 31.
MILO
Is it? Heh—I never bother with that business stuff. I'll get someone to look into it. Let me get you another glass of champagne.
NINA enters with a bouquet of flowers.
NINA
Milo. Me old darlin'.
(kisses him)
I'm here for a slightly premature celebration.
MILO
Mm-hm.
NINA
Remember the information that I imparted to you about my imminent megabucks deal in the States? Well, it's about to come to fruition. You know I want you to be my right-hand man.
The doorbell chimes. One of MILO's ASSISTANTS goes to the door.
NINA
We're going to blow Vanity Fair out of the fucking water, darling. I've a friend at The New Yorker who says that Tina is shitting herself.
REGINA
Oh!
NINA
Regina?!
REGINA
Hi.
SISSY enters the room in a bathrobe and carries a bottle of champagne.
SISSY
Oh, oh, oh. I'm sorry. I thought this was Gerard Depardieu's suite.
MILO shrugs.
INT - MORGUE - AUTOPSY ROOM - NIGHT
ISABELLA comes to see OLIVIER's corpse. The door opens and SIMONE enters. She stops at the doorway when she sees ISABELLA. They look at each other but say nothing. They each know quite well who the other is. INSPECTORS TANTPIS and FORGET are there.
TANTPIS
Qu'est-ce que c'est que ça? (What's that?)
NURSE
C'est de la merde de chien. (Dog shit.)
TANTPIS
Ca porte bonheur. (It brings good luck.)
NURSE
Surtout si c'est le pied gauche.
ISABELLA
(to SIMONE)
He never looked better.
ISABELLA leaves.
TANTPIS
Allons Forget! (Let's go!)
SIMONE has a moment alone with OLIVIER's body.
EXT - MORGUE - PARKING AREA - NIGHT
Several REPORTERS are waiting. SIMONE comes out and is surrounded by the PRESS She

142

refuses to answer their questions, but they hold her there.

SKY TV REPORTER
Isabella de la Fontaine, my condolences. Would you please answer a few questions? It's no secret here in Paris that your husband was involved with Simone Lo.

ISABELLA
Where's the car?

SKY TV REPORTER
How do you feel about that right now? Is it true that your husband was in financial turmoil?

TANTPIS and FORGET come out of the morgue. TANTPIS steps in dog shit.

SKY TV REPORTER
Did you know your husband had enemies? What are you going to do now?

ISABELLA gets in her car.

SKY TV REPORTER
Thank you, Mrs., thank you Mrs. de la Fontaine, my condolences.
(to CREW)
Okay, come here. Move, move, move, move. This is Sandra de la Notte reporting.

SIMONE comes out of the morgue and heads for her car.

SKY TV REPORTER
There she is! Simone Lowenthal. Come here, come here. Mrs. Lowenthal! Simone Lo! Mrs. Lo, please could you please answer a few questions.

SIMONE
Please, leave me alone.

SKY TV REPORTER
For Sky News please. What was your relationship with the victim of the murder?

SIMONE
Please, please leave me alone.

SKY TV REPORTER
Did you have quarrels with his wife? Could you please tell me about your collection, please? What was your relationship with the victim?

SIMONE
Why don't you ask his widow?

SKY TV REPORTER
Who do you think could have done such a horrible thing?

INT - JOE & ANNE'S ROOM - NIGHT
JOE watches a Sky News TV report of OLIVIER's death. He is on the phone with his news bureau in Washington, calling in his report.

SKY TV REPORTER (ON TV)
These bizarre circumstances have cast a strange pall...

JOE
(on phone)
These bizarre circumstance have cast a strange pall over fashion week here in Paris...

SKY TV REPORTER (ON TV)
Where it's difficult to eclipse...

ANNE looks at JOE, appalled by his lack of journalistic ethics.

JOE
(on phone)
Where it's difficult to eclipse the epic drama of the Prêt-à-Porter. Ironically, the controversial figure at the center of it all has done just that.

SKY TV REPORTER (ON TV)
This is Sandra de la Notte, Sky-TV.

JOE
(on phone)
That's it. Well, I'll call with something on the coroner's report tomorrow. Yeah, well, fuck you too.
(He slams down the phone.)

INT - GRAND HOTEL - MISC. ROOM #1 - NIGHT
A TV SET IS ON. CAMERA PULLS BACK to see SERGEI in a hotel robe, altering JOE'S suit with a small hand sewing machine. He is a master tailor. When he sees ISABELLA on TV he stops his work and watches. He becomes very sentimental.

144

SERGEI
Isabella! Isabella...
(sings)
Abat jour...
INT - JACK & DANE'S APARTMENT- NIGHT
DANE is on the phone with her sister, KIKI. She is dressed to go out.
DANE
You know, they said it was a man who murdered him. I would've guessed his wife.
INT - KIKI'S BATHROOM
KIKI's side of the conversation.
KIKI
Please. Simone's better off without him anyway.
DANE
So's his wife.
JACK comes into KIKI's bathroom, sniffs her underwear.
JACK
Kiki!
DANE
Did you ever sleep with him?
KIKI·
Get out of here. No, I wouldn't do that to Simone. Why, are you trying to tell me something?
DANE
Not quite. I have to go. I'm cooking.
KIKI
Okay.
DANE
Bye.
KIKI
Bye.
KIKI hangs up and joins JACK who is waiting for her on the bed.
JACK
Who's on the phone?
KIKI
Only your wife.
(They kiss.)
INT - GRAND HOTEL - JOE & ANNE'S ROOM - NIGHT
JOE sets up the room service cart for dinner. KITTY POTTER is on TV.
JOE
Want some wine?
ANNE
No. I shouldn't.
The phone rings. ANNE answers.
ANNE
Hello? Yes, this is Anne Eisenhower. Yes. Yes—well, you know, it's just completely unacceptable, I'm afraid, because I have to have my bag. Well, I-I-I filled out the form and everything's there just—if you could just please keep looking. Thank you. Thank you very much.
KITTY
(on TV)
...guaranteeing you that I'm going to bring you a drama.
ANNE walks to the room service cart that JOE has set up. She picks up a glass of wine and chugs it.
JOE
I thought you said you didn't drink.
ANNE
I said I shouldn't drink.
JOE pours himself another glass of wine.
JOE
Cheers.

ANNE

Thank you.

ANNE takes the glass and drinks. JOE pours himself another glass. ANNE takes that glass and drinks.

ANNE

Um—these French really know how to make wine.

ANNE takes the next glass that JOE pours for himself.

INT - PHOTO STUDIO - NIGHT

FIONA is setting up her designer photo shoot. As many REAL DESIGNERS as we can gather are there for the famous group photo, milling around and gossiping while the shoot is being prepared. BIANCO and ROMNEY are both there with VIOLETTA and REGGIE. MILO's entourage does all the setting-up work. MILO is cool.

FIONA

Just go ahead without Simone.

MILO

You guys, I'm fed up waitin'. I'm gonna do this now, all right?

ASSISTANT #1

Yeah.

MILO

You ready?

ASSISTANT #1

You charged?

ASSISTANT #2

I'm ready.

MILO walks from behind the camera to the GROUP OF DESIGNERS.

MILO

Hi. So hope you're all well. You look lovely. I'm just going to do this shot now, okay? Uh—the important thing is, I'm gonna count to three. When I say three, that's when the shot is gonna be so I just want you to keep your eyes wide open, you know, no blinking. Okay. Focus on the camera when I say three, all right. Here we go.

He walks back behind his camera, muttering.

MILO

Thank you, thank you, thank you, thank you...

SIMONE rushes in with PILAR.

SIMONE

Sorry I'm late.

MILO

Winnie, put her in the center.

SIMONE

No, no, no.

(to DESIGNERS)

Sorry.

WINNIE and PILAR put SIMONE in the center then step back behind the camera. Finally the shot is ready, and MILO steps in to click the camera.

MILO

Hi, Simone. Now, on the count of three I want you to look over here. All right?

SIMONE

Okay, sorry.

MILO

Okay.

(to ASSISTANT)

Excuse me. I'm trying to...

(to the DESIGNERS)

And again, over here, please. One, two, three.

(MILO takes the photograph.)

EXT - MORNING IN PARIS - DAY

Establishing SHOT of city ending up on the LOUVRE pyramid. CROWDS are pouring into the pyramid. SERGEI, in JOE's tailored, checkered sport jacket walks toward the pyramid until he steps in dog shit. He stops to clean his shoe. FIONA rushes past on her way to KITTY and the FAD CREW.

KITTY

This is Kitty Potter reporting Live on the first day of the Fall 1994 Paris Collections. The remarkably well-preserved crowd of fashion folk you see around me look as though they're about to break into the "Bonjour Paris" number from Funny Face, don't they? But in reality, they're headed for the trenches. Fashion, my friends, is war. A week from now these editors, journalists, photographers, and retailers will wear their battle scars much as they do their huge Prada handbags and their Vivienne Westwood platform shoes—as chic accessories. Even a wisp of iron like Regina Krumm, the Lilliputian editor of Elle magazine, is here for the blood sport. With eighty-six collections to view, vision blurs and judgment is occasionally impaired. Wearing dark glasses can't stop it either. There will be great lapses in taste, but there will also be dazzling moments of rare beauty. And I'll be everywhere at once, that's Kitty Potter keeping you posted.

INT - LACROIX SHOW - RUNWAY/AUDIENCE - DAY

PHOTOGRAPHERS are lining both sides of the runway. VIPs, real and fictional, are seated in the front rows. Among them are SLIM, CLINT (with a beautiful MODEL) and JACK who are sitting with MILO, MAJOR, SISSY, REGINA, and NINA, who are there with their assistants, VIVIENE, CRAIG, and JEAN-PIERRE. There is one empty prime seat with the name OLIVIER DE LA FONTAINE on it. KITTY, SOPHIE, and the FAD CREW are also there. The lights dim. The music starts. The show begins.

INT - GRAND HOTEL - JOE & ANNE'S ROOM - DAY

The bed is an absolute mess, there is food all over the place, clothes and sheets included. ANNE goes to the door in a hotel robe, carrying her dirty clothes. A VALET is there to take her laundry.

ANNE

That's got a bad stain on it.

As she hands the valet her dirty clothes, JOE throws out his dirty clothes from the bathroom.

INT - LACROIX SHOW - DAY

LACROIX takes the runway

INT - LACROIX SHOW - BACKSTAGE - DAY

A flurry of activity is taking place after the show. MODELS are changing into their street clothes. Our CAST MEMBERS who are there join in the CROWD congratulating CHRISTIAN LACROIX. KITTY is there with her CREW.

KITTY

Whither the couturier in his metier you ask. And I answer right here backstage at Christian Lacroix, the artist from Arles, the savior of Ready-to-Wear deluxe. Christian it was such a beautiful collection and so perfect. Uh—what was perfect for you this morning?

LACROIX

Perfection for me? It doesn't exist. Never. In fashion, we are never satisfied.

KITTY

Well, let me ask you something? The photo prints of the models and the faces were just wonderful. How did you come up with that idea?

LACROIX

Because now in fashion is—uh—starting from the media, from magazines, and from models, and I wanted to put them in the street. Because I want people to be a little disturbed, and they don't know where is reality: fashion, and magazine, media, models, girls, real girls... I wanted to mix all of that.

EXT - CLOTHING BOUTIQUE - DAY

LOUISE has just made a purchase and exits the shop.

INT - SIMONE LO'S ATELIER - DAY

FIONA is interviewing JACK.

FIONA

Is she going ahead with the show?

JACK

Well, of course. It is our business after all.

FIONA

Will she actually be there herself?

PILAR leads out a group of MOURNERS as SONIA and NATHALIE RYKIEL enter.

PILAR

C'est très gentil d'être venu. (It's nice of you to come.)

NATHALIE

Comment va Simone? (How's Simone?)

PILAR

Ça va, Nathalie.

NATHALIE

On est desolé. (We are so sorry.)

PILAR

Merci. Au revoir.

MOURNERS

Au revoir.

NATHALIE

(to MOURNERS)

Au revoir. On se voit après. (We'll see each other afterwards.)

INT - SIMONE'S PRIVATE OFFICE

PILAR brings the RYKIELS to SIMONE.

PILAR

C'est Sonya et Nathalie qui sont ici. (Sonya and Nathalie are here.)

SIMONE

C'est gentil d'être venu. (Nice of you to come.)

SONYA

On s'assoit deux minutes. On est venu juste t'embrasser. (We'll sit two minutes. We just came to give you a hug.)

INT - GRAND HOTEL - JOE & ANNE'S ROOM - DAY

ANNE is leaving a message on her newspaper's answering machine.

ANNE

Bernell, it's Anne, and I'm just calling to say everything is great in Paris. I'm in the hotel. I got all the schedules, all the invitations. And so that's it. If you need to call me, just remember the time change. Okay, bye.

ANNE hangs up the phone. The doorbell rings. JOE comes out of the bathroom as ANNE opens the door. A waiter is there with a breakfast cart.

WAITER #1

Bonjour Madame. Bonjour Monsieur. Votre signature, s'il vous plaît.

JOE signs.

WAITER #1

Merci. Au revoir.

The TV is on with KITTY talking about the opening of the Prêt-à-Porter. JOE changes the channel to French basketball. ANNE looks at him.

ANNE

You know, this is a really unusual circumstance and... I just—I just hope that you can forget about last night. Um—I have a little problem with alcohol. And um...

JOE is engrossed in the basketball game.

ANNE

Excuse me? Hello. Hi. Um—I just—I hope that you can be a gentleman, and that we can just say what happened last night never happened. Okay?

JOE

Sure, no problem.

He slurps his coffee.

ANNE

No problem, really.

JOE

Yeah, whatever you want.

ANNE

Just forgotten.

(snaps her fingers)

Like that. It's so easy.

JOE

Yeah.

ANNE

PRÊT à PORTER
de R. ALTMAN
Photo : E. GEORGES
Date : 11/4/94

23

That's great.
JOE
Well... what? Am I supposed to be crushed or something?
ANNE
No. No. No! This is—this is great. This is just great.
(throws an orange at him)
You know. Yup, that's great...
She snatches the TV remote, changes the channel to a shaving commercial and locks herself in the bathroom. JOE chases her.
JOE
Aw, c'mon. Don't change the channel. C'mon. Hey, hey, hey. Aw c'mon, now gimme back the channel changer.
INT - CHRISTIAN DIOR SHOW
Runway show.
INT - SIMONE'S PRIVATE OFFICE - DAY
CORT ROMNEY and VIOLETTA enter to offer their condolences to SIMONE.
CORT ROMNEY
Simone, condolences
VIOLETTA
Condolences.
SIMONE
That's very nice, but isn't it your show today?
CORT ROMNEY
Oh... that's not important. Our concern is for our friends. Business will take care of business.
VIOLETTA
I am so sorry for you. I can feel your pain.
CORT ROMNEY
Simone, I have to be honest with you. Olivier and I were never great friends, but you know that. But to be murdered, strangled by a maniac... it makes my flesh crawl. But you, you poor, poor dear. You are truly the bravest woman in Christendom.
SIMONE
Oh, you're so kind. Really.
INT - DIOR SHOW - BACKSTAGE
KITTY interviews the DESIGNER in the rush of the post-show party.
KITTY
Oh, where's my crew? Where's my camera? Oh, there you go... I'm standing here with the handsomest man I know: Mr. Gianfranco Ferré, the Italian designer in residence at the venerated, old French house of Christian Dior. Gianfranco, bravissimo.
GIANFRANCO
Thanks a lot, Kitty. You speak Italian so well.
KITTY
Such refinement. What inspired you this time?
GIANFRANCO
Well, it's the energy that a woman needs—uh—in these times. I try to do my best. I love women. I like to make fantasies with women. But—uh—I always figure what she does, how she moves, which way she can move... But she can make her wardrobe with different pieces without throwing them away season after season. Show she can make her own new traditions with the freedom that she needs.
INT - SIMONE'S PRIVATE OFFICE - DAY
CY BIANCO and REGGIE enter.
CY BIANCO
Simone! I know this has been a great shock to you.
REGGIE
Condoléances.
CY BIANCO
You lost your man. And I know you're not gonna want to hear what I've got to say, but, Olivier, he was not a nice man. There I've said it, it's over, it's done, it's finished, it's gone. I mean, I could tell you stories about him that would make you want to scream. God knows you're better off without that man. I mean, he did not deserve you. No, no, no,

no, no, no, no. He did not deserve you. Believe me, you'll get over him. You're a strong woman. Right?
SIMONE
Yes. I'm a strong woman.
INT - MIYAKE BOUTIQUE - DAY
LOUISE gets out of a taxi.
LOUISE
Okay. Merci beaucoup. A bientôt. Keep the change, mon ami.
LOUISE enters the shop, looks at a green dress. A sales clerk approaches.
LOUISE
Hi. Um—do you have this in larger sizes? This green. It's beautiful.
SALES CLERK
Yes, it is a medium.
LOUISE
A fourteen or an eighteen. A big... It stretches, right?
SALES CLERK
Yes. Is this for you?
LOUISE shrugs.
INT - MIYAKE SHOW
The runway show at Miyake. SERGEI is wandering in the CROWD.
INT - GRAND HOTEL - JOE & ANNE'S ROOM - DAY
JOE's on the phone. He tries his best to speak French. ANNE watches the Miyake show on TV and takes notes.
JOE
The number of the coroner. Look no... J'ai besoin le nombre de telephone de coroner, l'homme de morte. (I need the telephone figure of coroner, the man of dead.) No, no,no. Monsieur, je suis morte. Ou est je suis? (Mister, I am dead. Where is I am?) No, no, no. Monsieur. Monsieur, imagine... je suis morte. Ou est... (I am dead. Where is...)
He suddenly sees his checkered, sport coat when SERGEI passes by a camera.
JOE
Hey, that's my jacket.
ANNE
That's your jacket.
JOE
That was my jacket. That guy had my jacket on. That must've been the guy that took—took my—my suitcase.
ANNE
Oh, so Issey Miyake stole your suitcase.
JOE
No, not... The checkered thing. It was my jacket.
ANNE
I don't know that Issey Miyake is really your way to go. Checkered. I think Jean C. Penné is more your designer.
On TV, KITTY interviews ISSEY MIYAKE backstage.
KITTY (ON TV)
I loved it. It was wonderful. Tell us about those marvelous, marvelous hats.
ISSEY (ON TV)
Well, it's about what we can find from our daily life...
INT - SIMONE LO'S ATELIER - DAY
INSPECTORS TANTPIS and FORGET question SIMONE. PILAR and a couple of MODELS are in another section of the room.
TANTPIS
Nous avons eté extrêmement surpris l'inspecteur Forget et moi même en commençant notre enquête de nous apercevoir que la victime etait quelqu'un de très important dans le milieu de la mode, votre milieu... Et que de plus il ne semblait pas tres apprecié. (The inspector and I were very surprised to learn that the victim was an important figure in the fashion world. And that he was not very well liked.)
PILAR brings a MODEL to SIMONE. SIMONE changes the MODEL's blouse. The INSPECTORS are uncomfortable for the few seconds that the MODEL is naked.
SIMONE

C'est vrai, il n'etait pas très aimé. C'était le President de la Chambre Syndicale mais personne ne l'aimait dans la mode.(It's true. He wasn't well liked. He was the president of the fashion council.) Ça c'est trop grand. (Nobody liked him.)
TANTPIS
Même vous, Madame? (Even you, Madame?)
SIMONE
Non, je ne l'aimais pas beaucoup. (No, I didn't like him very much.)
TANTPIS
Mais pourtant, on dit qu'il etait votre amant.(But they say he was your lover.)
SIMONE
Cela n'a rien a voir. Non, ce n'était pas quelqu'un d'exceptionnel. (What's that got to do with anything. He wasn't a very nice person.)
On TV, is a SKY TV news report.
SKY TV REPORTER
...sycophant and purple panderer, storming out of the Pamela Harriman dinner party at the American Embassy only last Tuesday, prompting the New York Post headline: "Simone... how Lo can you go." Jack, son of the designer, lost control of the business in 1990...
During this, JACK enters with SLIM and CLINT.
JACK
Stay here just for one moment. Pilar!
PILAR, who has been working with a MODEL, turns to see JACK.
PILAR
Simone!
SIMONE walks over to greet the newcomers.
SLIM
Simone, oh, I know this must be a very awkward time for you, but I so wanted to introduce Clint Lammereaux to you. Clint is a gigantic fan of yours.
CLINT
In Texas we think of Simone Lowenthal the same way we think of longhorns.
SIMONE
Oh, how nice.
INSPECTORS TANTPIS and FORGET are still standing in the doorway, waiting.
TANTPIS
La victime ne semble pas très aimée, cela pourrait faciliter notre enquête. (Everyone seems to hate the victim... that should make our investigation easier.)
FORGET
Oui, ou la rendre plus difficile. (Or more difficult.)
TANTPIS
Vous êtes en train de me contredire, Forget? (Are you contradicting me, Forget?)
FORGET
Non, Monsiuer. J'essaye de vous aider. C'est tout. (No, sir. I'm only trying to help.)
TANTPIS
N'en faites rien. (Well, don't.)
JACK
Clint, come over here.
SIMONE glances at SLIM's feet and notices she's wearing two different-colored shoes.
SIMONE
How interesting?
SLIM
What's interesting?
SIMONE
Your shoes. Is that new?
SLIM looks at her shoes.
SLIM
Oh no, I've had them for years. Speaking of shoes. Clint has a gift for you.
CLINT opens a box and presents SIMONE with a pair of cowboy boots with the "Lo" logo.
CLINT
Made in Texas by Texans.
SIMONE is more curious than impressed.
SIMONE

Oh, you put my logo on these boots? But who gave you permission?

INT - CORT ROMNEY'S SHOW - AUDIENCE

Everyone is clamoring for a seat. ISABELLA enters and the press goes wild, screaming her name and taking pictures. ISABELLA arrives at her seat and finds NINA has stolen it.

NINA

Sorry, I'm in your seat. My condolences.

ISABELLA

Thank you.

KITTY POTTER is in the lobby and attempts an interview.

KITTY

Nicoli?

TRUSSARDA

Hi, Kitty. Nice to see you.

KITTY

Nice to see you. I don't think we've seen each other since the Volpi Ball in Venice.

TRUSSARDA

Yes, I remember.

KITTY

Remember?

TRUSSARDA

Yes.

KITTY

What's new? What going on at Trussarda's? How 'bout doing a little interview with us? We're rolling? Hi, this is Kitty Potter live in Paris with Nicoli Trussarda, a world master of Italian leather and fashion. Tell us about the new Trussarda attitude, Nicoli.

TRUSSARDA

No interview, Kitty. Thank you.

KITTY

Nicoli, just one word.

TRUSSARDA

No, thank you.

KITTY

Just one word.

TRUSSARDA

Ciao.

He walks away.

KITTY

Shit.

INT - CORT ROMNEY'S SHOW - BACKSTAGE - DAY

There is a flurry of activity. VIOLETTA is in a corner on a telephone speaking to REGGIE.

VIOLETTA

(In French)

Ça m'excite tellement. (You excite me so...) Il faut que je te vois. (I want you so much...) Je veux que tu me défonces jusqu'au bout, je veux que tu m'exploses. (I want you to make me burst.)

CORT ROMNEY comes up behind her and startles her. He's manic.

CORT ROMNEY

What are you doing talking on the telephone at a time like this. For God's sake, Violetta. We're about to start.

INT - CY BIANCO'S ATELIER - DAY

REGGIE is on the phone with someone who hangs up on him. REGGIE looks at the dead phone and hangs it up. We know it's VIOLETTA.

INT - ROMNEY BACKSTAGE - DAY

VIOLETTA

I was only talking to my mother.

CORT ROMNEY

Your mother? Your mother is in Algeria. You're talking to Africa at a time like this?

VIOLETTA

Well, she's sick.

INT - CY BIANCO'S ATELIER - DAY

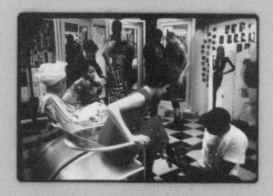

CY BIANCO is working on a MODEL with a couple of ASSISTANTS. REGGIE approaches.
REGGIE
It's beautiful.
CY BIANCO
Like that?
REGGIE
I like that.
CY BIANCO
It's nice.
REGGIE
This is your best one yet, you know. No doubt.
CY BIANCO
Thanks Eve.
REGGIE
No doubt about it.
CY BIANCO
Who're you talking to on the phone?
REGGIE
Who me? Oh...
CY BIANCO
Yeah, yeah, just now you were talking to somebody on the phone, right?
REGGIE
Yes, I was, I was.
(a MODEL passes by)
She's cute...
CY BIANCO
Yeah, well who were you talking to on the phone right now?
REGGIE
Yes...
CY BIANCO
Who was that?
REGGIE
(whispering into his ear)
You know what? I love you when you are jealous.
INT - ROMNEY AUDIENCE - DAY
KITTY walks to her seat in the front row. The man sitting next to her seat, HARRY
BELAFONTE, is leaning over her chair.
KITTY
'Scuse me. I think—I do believe...
(she recognizes HARRY BELAFONTE)
Oh! I do believe... Well, hello!
BELAFONTE
Hello.
KITTY
How are you? My name's Kitty Potter.
BELAFONTE
Nice to see you.
KITTY
Nice to see you as well!
INT - ROMNEY SHOW - RUNWAY
The show begins...
INT - JOE & ANNE'S ROOM - DAY
JOE and ANNE are still in their hotel robes. ANNE is asleep on the couch. JOE watches a
news report about OLIVIER's death. DESIGNERS are being interviewed about their reactions.
SONIA RYKIEL (ON TV)
I'm very upset. It was—it's so sudden, and so also I'm very sad for Simone.
CLAUDE MONTANA (ON TV)
The reaction I have is—uh—sort of personal, and I can't talk about it on TV.
CY BIANCO (ON TV)
I'm not happy. I'm just—I just think that the earth does not cry...

JEAN-PAUL GAULTIER
Uh—I saw him just like two weeks ago. He was—uh...
ANNE wakes up and looks at her watch and checks her schedule.
ANNE
I have a show starting in a couple of minutes.
INT - CORT ROMNEY'S SHOW - DAY
SERGEI is in the audience. He passes right under the noses of INSPECTORS TANTPIS and
FORGET. At the finale of the show, CORT ROMNEY takes the runway walk with his MODELS. All
the AUDIENCE gets up, ready to file backstage.
INT - CORT ROMNEY'S SHOW - BACKSTAGE - DAY
EVERYONE crowds around CORT and VIOLETTA ROMNEY. The journalists, SLIM, CLINT, MAJOR,
take turns congratulating him. The MODELS are getting dressed. KITTY, SOPHIE, and the FAD
interview CORT ROMNEY. VIOLETTA is by his side.
KITTY
Here's the designer and his wife, Violetta, reveling in post-show euphoria.
Congratulations.
MAJOR
It was great! It was fabulous! This world will never see it again!
KITTY
(to MAJOR)
Thank you. Congratulations.
NINA
(to ROMNEY)
Hello, darling. Unbelievable.
KITTY
What about the shapes? Are they feminine?
ROMNEY
Well, Kitty. I think that my ideal woman has a bust, a waist, and hips, but she is not
shy with her shoulders. I think—I think shoulders are very fresh again. And, of course,
legs. She doesn't have to have legs... it's wonderful if she does. Don't you think?
REGINA walks up to MILO and puts a note in his pocket.
REGINA
'Scuse me. I'm putting this in your pocket. I think you should read it, and then I think
you should call me.
She turns to leave and almost bumps right into ALBERTINE's protruding belly.
REGINA
Oh my lord, Albertine!
INT - CORT ROMNEY'S SHOW - LOBBY - DAY
KITTY and the FAD CREW burst out of the doors followed by the rest of the ROMNEY
AUDIENCE.
KITTY
God, it's so hot in there.
Next comes HARRY BELAFONTE who is instantly surrounded by reporters who scream out his
name. KITTY sees him.
KITTY
Oh!
(re: her microphone)
Gimme. Gimme, gimme, gimme.
SOPHIE
Mr. Belafonte...
KITTY
Harry!
SOPHIE
Can you do an interview with Kitty Potter?
KITTY
Hey!
BELAFONTE
How are you?
KITTY
Remember me?

BELAFONTE
Yes, I remember.
KITTY
Could we do that interview now? Do you mind?
(to her CREW)
We're rolling? I'm standing here with a gentleman who needs no introduction, I believe.
BELAFONTE
Hi.
KITTY
What brings you to Paris?
BELAFONTE
Well, we're doing a film about...
While this is going on, ISABELLA reaches the entrance to the dressing room, the PRESS realizes that she is there and turns to her. At the same time she sees SERGEI face-to-face. He smiles "hello" and ISABELLA faints. KITTY pushes her way to the scene and starts to report.
KITTY
Oh! Oh my God! Bedlam! Bedlam has broken out backstage at Cort Romney's show. Isabella de la Fontaine has fainted. She has lost consciousness.
(to someone in the crowd)
Is she dead?
SOMEONE
No, she just fainted.
KITTY
She isn't dead. She is not dead. I—I don't know what her condition is. Has somebody called a medic?
INT - JOE & ANNE'S ROOM
ANNE is taking fashion notes from a TV report. JOE answers the door. A WAITER enters with a bottle of champagne.
WAITER
Excusez moi.
JOE
Um—I didn't order that.
WAITER
Oh. C'est un cadeau de la direction, Monsieur. (A gift from the management.)
JOE
What?
WAITER
C'est un cadeau de la direction, Monsieur.
JOE
Oh, yeah. Listen, listen. You know where my laundry is? Lavez moi.
ANNE calls out to JOE without turning around.
ANNE
Laundry?
JOE
Not quite.
JOE begins to open up the bottle. He hesitates a moment, speculating, then pops the cork. ANNE smiles at the sound.
INT - CORT ROMNEY'S SHOW - FIRST AID STATION ENTRANCE - DAY
KITTY gives a report on the condition of ISABELLA.
KITTY
(flustered)
Isabella de la Fontaine is in stable condition, stable condition. She's being examined here right now—right now—by a team of fashion doctors here at the site of Cort Romney's show...
TANTPIS and FORGET are watching ISABELLA.
TANTPIS
Le stress. Elle est stressé. (Stress. She is under great stress.)
FORGET
Ou alors elle a vu quelque chose ou quelqu'un qu'elle ne s'atendait pas a voir. (Or

perhaps she saw someone in the crowd she did not expect to see.)
TANTPIS
Qui ne s'attendait elle pas a voir?
(Who would she expect not to see?)
FORGET
Je ne sais pas. Peut-être l'homme qui etait avec son mari quand il a été tué.
(I don't know. Perhaps she saw the man who was with her husband when he died.)
During this time ISABELLA has recovered and is with FIONA.
KITTY
It was a fainting, which took place here today, just days after her husband's death by
strangulation, her first public appearance in, well, twenty-five years! Madame de la
Fontaine had just rocked the fashion world by taking her husband's symbolically vacant
seat in the front row, wearing what fashion observers could only speculate to be a
black, vintage Dior dress. Until his untimely death, Olivier de la Fontaine was
commonly known to be involved with Simone Lowenthal, for most of the duration of his
marriage. Oh! Here she is right now, and she's looking mighty fine to me. Who made your
dress?
TANTPIS and FORGET are still watching.
TANTPIS
Comment ça, assassiné? Mais bien sûr qu'il a été assassiné sinon nous ne serions pas dans
le coup? Vous voyez trop de films americains, mon garçon. (If he were murdered? Of
course, he was murdered. Otherwise, why would we be on this case? You've been seeing too
many American movies, my friend.)
INT - PARIS BOUTIQUE - DAY
LOUISE shops for accessories.
LOUISE
Porte-jartelles. Porte-jartelles de dentelle? (Garter belt. Garter belt of lace?) Et
guepiere. Oui, oui. (And camisole?) Et avez-vous soutient gorge de dentelle? (And do you
have a lace bra?) Avec pe-petites culottes? (with cute panties?) Oui, ooh, très bien. La
ceinture. (The belt.) Very nice accessories. Yes, very nice. Accessoires. Accessoires.
(Accessories. Accessories.)
INT - CY BIANCO'S - ATELIER - DAY
CY BIANCO is on the phone.
CY BIANCO
No, he doesn't even suspect, but he's such a bitch. I mean, he's snooping though all my
things, he's going through all my pockets. He says we have to be careful. Of course, I'm
going to get rid of him. I just have to wait until after the collection. Okay?
INT - ROMNEY'S OFFICE - SAME MOMENT
CORT ROMNEY is on the phone with CY BIANCO.
ROMNEY
I love you.
BIANCO (over phone)
I love you, too.
ROMNEY is so overcome, he drops the phone.
INT - GAULTIER SHOW - DAY
SLIM, CLINT, and JACK; SISSY, REGINA, NINA with their ASSISTANTS; MAJOR and FIONA; and
KITTY and SOPHIE. SERGEI enters, stands in the CROWD; he still wears JOE's checkered
sport coat.
INT - JOE & ANNE'S ROOM - DAY
KITTY's report continues on a TV set. The champagne bottle lies empty on the floor. JOE
and ANNE are under a lot of covers. We hear giggling sounds as they make love.
INT - GAULTIER SHOW - BACKSTAGE - DAY
JEAN-PAUL GAULTIER is greeted by well-wishers.
GAULTIER
Did you like the show?
SISSY
It really was. I loved the show.
GAULTIER
How are you? Did you like the show?
SLIM

@ IMAPRESS 4033003

PH: YANNIS VLAMOS OR

@ IMAPRESS 4033003

PH: YANNIS VLAMOS OR

"PRET A PORTER"
UN FILM DE R.ALTMAN

Très bien. Merveilleux.
NINA
So you are my hero.
GAULTIER
Thank you all. Did you like the show?
REGINA claps her approval.
KITTY
Could we do a little thing here? Do you mind?
GAULTIER
Okay.
KITTY
Okay. Thank you. Thank you. Anyway, I'm with the man who gave us fetish fashions, he gave us pierced nipples and uh—oh, I can't say that. I don't think I can say that. Uh—anyway, tell me your ideas on beauty. Would you please?
GAULTIER
I think there is not only one idea of beauty, I think there is a lot of different kinds of beauty. Uh—it's exactly what I try to show in my different collection. You know that there is different people coming from different parts that does not have the profile, the Greek profile, something like that—that can be beautiful. I try to show like a kind of tolerance where is that, you know, to be different you can be and to be proud about it and to live like that.
KITTY
Well, you heard it here from the wizard of our Oz: Jean-Paul Gaultier. And I'm Kitty Potter with FAD.
INT - REGINA'S SUITE - DAY
REGINA is alone with MILO. She pours him a cup of tea.
MILO
So, I got your note.
REGINA
Well, I sort of had to resort to that, you know. You're so hard to get to with all those people around you. Would you like cream or milk with your tea?
MILO
No, I don't like tea.
REGINA
Ah! Well, that's fine. We can just get right to the point, Milo. May I call you Milo, Mr. O'Branagan?
MILO
Oh, sure. Love the way you say it. Sounds just like me old mother. Warms the cockles in my heart.
REGINA
You know what I want to talk about, don't you?
MILO
Haven't the foggiest. But I love surprises.
REGINA
And I love your work. I want you to sign with Elle. I'll get you everything you want. I'd stake my job on it.
MILO
Would you, now?
REGINA
Yes, I would. And more than that.
MILO
What could be more than that, Miss Krumm.
REGINA
Well, let's see... uh—I would get down on my hands and knees if I thought it would help.
MILO
Ha! You never know, it might help.
MILO and REGINA share an uncomfortable laugh.
REGINA
I beg your pardon?
MILO

Oh, you said would it help if you got down on your hands and knees, and I said, well, you never know, might help.
REGINA
It might help. And you think I won't do that, don't you? Just you watch me.
REGINA kneels before MILO.
REGINA
Does that make you happy?
He whips out a spy camera and begins clicking off shots. REGINA is horrified. She slips and falls down. He continues shooting.
REGINA
What the hell are you doing? You goddamn idiot, cut that out. Get out! Get the hell out of my room! Aaaah! You know what you are? You are a goddamn amateur. You are the fucking Irish flavor of the month. Zap!
INT - SIMONE LO'S ATELIER - SUNRISE
SIMONE arrives to find that the some of the show clothes have disappeared. She turns to PILAR.
SIMONE
Where are my clothes?
PILAR
Jack took them.
SIMONE
What do you mean, he took them?
PILAR
Mi racomando Simone, non ti inrabbiare. Tuo figlio no esta bene. (Don't ask. You're son is no good.)
SIMONE
Okay, Pilar. Okay. Where are the clothes?
PILAR
The Milo O'Branagan shoot.
INT - PHOTO STUDIO - HALLWAY - DAY
MILO arrives for a photo shoot. He steps in dog shit.
MILO
Aw... shit! Winnie!
INT - PHOTO STUDIO - DAY
PHOTOGRAPHIC ASSISTANTS are scurrying around a rented studio space, setting up for a shoot. SLIM, CLINT and JACK are standing around waiting for MILO, who is late. MODELS including DANE and KIKI are wearing Simone's clothes and cowboy boots waiting to start working. The "Lo" logo is prominently displayed as part of the shoot. MILO enters.
MILO
Get over here! What's going on? I've got dog shit all over me shoe! Who brought a dog in here?
SLIM
None of us.
CLINT
That's one of the reasons we wear these boots. In Texas, you're always stepping in somethin'.
MILO
Take it away and incinerate it. Good morning.
SLIM
Good morning, Milo.
JACK
(dropping something in Milo's pocket)
I brought a little present for you.
MILO
Listen—uh—could you clear out of here because I wanta get this thing done kinda fast, okay?
SLIM
Oh, okay. All right, Clint! Clint! C'mon, pay attention.
SLIM, CLINT and JACK leave the studio and watch the shoot from a glass booth.
MILO

Okay, let's do this. Hi. Bonjour. Good morning. Ça va. How you doing, Anne? Hey, Kiki. Could you take your positions, please?
DANE
Sure...
MILO
I'll just have a look at this. You got—Constant! You got the Polaroids?
CONSTANT
Here you are.
MILO
You know, what are we selling? Hats or boots? Get the hats off. That's not bad, it looks all right, actually. Uh—okay. So, listen you're all looking gorgeous and talented and full of sexual allure and all that kinda stuff. It's just as well because the clothes are kinda boring, and these boots were made for walking.
(begins shooting)
Okay... Over here, please... Heads up, please... Chin up... Over here, yeah, we're doing fine... Okay, imagine you're walking around in fucking Texas or someplace like that...
JACK, CLINT, and SLIM are watching.
JACK
This is so fucking now. you know.
MILO
Okay, you're John Wayne and you hate the camera... Okay, hold it... That's great... Think cowboy, you know... C'mon let's go. Chin up, please, Gamaliana... Yeah, very Randolph Scott...
JACK
So great...
MILO
I like that sullen look, you know. Okay, that's good. Hold it. Keep it there...
EXT - BOUTIQUE - DAY
LOUISE waves good-bye to the sales clerk.
LOUISE
Okay. Merci. Very, very nice. Au revoir. Okay, here's the taxi. Thank you. St. Germaine Du Prix, s'il vous plaît or St. Germaine Du Près. I don't know. Tout le bags. Woops! OK...
INT - GRAND HOTEL - SISSY'S ROOM - NIGHT
TV is on. SISSY, in a very décolleté dressing gown, is on the telephone. Behind her, VIVIENE gets dressed.
SISSY
2340, s'il vous plaît.
OPERATOR (on phone)
Pardon?
SISSY
Vingt-deux...
VIVIENE
Vingt-trois quarante.
SISSY
Vingt-trois quarante, please.
INT - MILO'S ROOM - NIGHT
TV is on here, as well. MILO's entourage examines slides and proof sheets on a desk. The phone rings.
ALAIN
Hello?
SISSY (on phone)
Milo O'Branagan, s'il vous plaît. Sissy Wanamaker, Harper's Bazaar.
ALAIN
Milo, it's the Wanamaker woman.
WINNIE
It's the woman from Harper's Bazaar, you know.
ALAIN
Hold on.
MILO puts on his sunglasses and takes the receiver.

MILO
Hi, Miss Wanamaker.
SISSY (on phone)
Sissy...
MILO
Sissy... I was just thinking about you.
SISSY (on phone)
You were? Well, I've been thinking about you too, Milo.
MILO
Have you now, Sissy?
SISSY (on phone)
Oh, yes, Milo. Yes, I have, I really have.
INT - GRAND HOTEL - JOE & ANNE'S ROOM - NIGHT
The TV is on. JOE and ANNE are in bed dancing under the sheets.
INT - GRAND HOTEL - SISSY'S ROOM - NIGHT
SISSY has arranged a bottle of champagne in an ice bucket. Two glasses are on the table.
She lights a candle. The room is dimly lit for a romantic evening. The doorbell rings.
VIVIENE
I'll get it!
SISSY
Oh, no you don't! I'll get the door. You get—you get the contract. Where is it?
VIVIENE
Okay! On the dresser.
SISSY
Okay, put it on the bed.
VIVIENE
Oh... yes. Anytime you need me, I'll be there, okay?
SISSY
Okay, just go. Just go.
Sissy takes a moment for herself, then opens the door. Milo stands there in his
sunglasses. We can see Viviene sneaking away in the background.
SISSY
Come on in. I'm surprised you're alone. Where's your entourage? Aren't you scared to be
alone in a room with me? I am. How 'bout some champagne.
MILO
You got a beer?
SISSY
A beer? Let me look. I like beer. Actually, I prefer it to champagne. But you know, when
in Rome... do as the Parisians do. I like a man who drinks beer. Actually, my father
drank it constantly. Don't forget, he was part Irish.
SISSY turns around to rummage through the refrigerator. MILO takes out his light meter to
get a footcandle reading. He's dissatisfied so he flicks on the lights. SISSY grabs two
bottles from the refrigerator and notices the bright light.
SISSY
Oh! How nice. But then, you do know about lighting, don't you. Shall we drink out of the
glasses or just drink out of the bottle.
MILO
Well, the bottle's fine.
SISSY
(notices label)
Oh—this is ale, but that's the same as beer, isn't it? Here's to us.
(they drink)
Shamrock. You don't know how much I admire you, Milo.
MILO
Do you now?
SISSY
Yes, I do.
MILO
Nice suite. Big bed.
SISSY

(rushes into bedroom)

Oh—you're driving me insane. I'm acting like a three-year-old teenager, for God's sake. I'm the editor of a fashion magazine, and you're the photographer. But I'm American, and I'm so noisy. And you're so quiet. So goddamn Irish. I mean, you're like "The Quiet Man." Oh, I don't know what to do. I want you to sign this contract, and I want you. So take me...

SISSY rips open her robe, baring her breasts. MILO whips out his spy camera and begins snapping photos.

SISSY

Oh! What are you doing?! Oh! God! What are you doing?! You son of a bitch, get out of here! Get out of here! Stop it! Viviene! Viviene! Oh, you son of a bitch!

EXT - BULGARI PARTY - NIGHT

KITTY is posted outside the famous Paris restaurant Le Doyen, where a glamorous party for BULGARI, the jeweler, is about to commence. The international fashion world is in attendance, including our cast members. There is confusion at the entrance since security is tight.

KITTY

This is Kitty Potter live from Paris. There's a kind of Mad Hatter magic in the air here tonight, judging by Nina Scant's magnificent millinery. This is just such an evening here at the elegant restaurant Le Doyen. A chic international crowd is gathering here to see a new collection of Haute Bijou from the celebrated designer Bulgari.

INT - GRAND HOTEL - HALLWAY - NIGHT

SERGEI passes by and bumps into MAJOR.

MAJOR

Will you open your eyes? Arrogant bastard...

SERGEI shows us that he has pickpocketed MAJOR's key.

EXT - BULGARI PARTY - NIGHT

KITTY

This is pure poetry here tonight, with some of the most beautiful jewels I have ever seen glittering everywhere you look—especially on the lovely throat of Isabella de la Fontaine. We haven't seen Isabella on the social circuit for some twenty-five years, and she's certainly made absolutely sure we won't miss her tonight!

INT - GRAND HOTEL - MAJOR'S ROOM - NIGHT

The TV is on broadcasting KITTY's report from the party. SERGEI begins rifling MAJOR's drawers, looking for something to wear. In one drawer he finds the pair of frilly skivvies. He looks at it and shrugs.

KITTY (ON TV)

Inside, we'll sit down to the sumptuous, contemporary cuisine that has earned Le Doyen its constellation of Michelin stars... but first, the dessert! Let's go inside and have a look at the jewelry, shall we?

INT - BULGARI PARTY - NIGHT

KITTY

I'm here with Paolo Bulgari, the third generation of a house which built its name on preserving and enhancing the style and workmanship of the Italian Renaissance, and the nineteenth-century Roman school of artisans. Paolo, the latest collection is a foray into the subtleties of porcelain. How did it evolve?

PAOLO

I tell you, about a couple of years ago...

Meanwhile, SLIM meets up with ELSA KLENSCH.

SLIM

I feel very at home here. It's so great to be in the middle of all this.

ELSA KLENSCH

Every six months, something different...

CRAIG

The car...

REGINA

You just stay with me.

SISSY

Viviene!

VIVIENE

Only a second!
KITTY
Oh, it's beautiful. Just marvelous. Thank you so much.
FIONA interviews NINA.
FIONA
How do you find the jewelry?
NINA
How do you find the jewelry? Uh—well, I usually shove my hand down the back of the sofa... hopefully, I come up with something.
NINA laughs at this.
FIONA
I'm talking about the Bulgari porcelain pieces.
NINA
Um—yes, I know you are. It's just such a boring question to ask. You know, unimaginative. Can't anyone ask anything serious every now and again.
FIONA
OK. How do you feel that 50 percent of the world's pollution is caused by the textile mills?
NINA is speechless.
INT - GRAND HOTEL - JOE & ANNE'S ROOM - NIGHT
JOE and ANNE sit on the sofa. They are wrapped up in bed sheets.
ANNE
The person I blame, and hate the most, is me, of course. I'm the one to blame. It's my fault. I know.
JOE
You shouldn't be so hard on yourself. It's my fault. I'm the one to blame. You couldn't help yourself.
ANNE
Oh, really?
JOE
Yeah, it wasn't fair of me.
ANNE
You're not all that irresistible, you know. I did have a little something to do with this decision. I assure you.
JOE
I didn't mean it that way.
ANNE
It was my choice. In fact, I'd say you had very little to do with this decision. I'd say you are simply a pawn in this game.
JOE
Game? Oh, that's great. You're a fuckin' piece of work, you know that. You telling me you just fall into bed with the first person who pours you a glass of wine?
ANNE
Oh, that's so typical of you to always go for the really cheap, low...
JOE
Always?! Always?! Listen, I don't know you. I just met you. I'm not your fucking husband!
ANNE
I'm not your fucking wife! Who do you think I am!
JOE
I'm trying to figure that out!
ANNE
Oh, are you?!
JOE
Yes, I am!
ANNE
Well, don't strain yourself!
JOE
Well, don't worry!
ANNE
I won't!

There's a pause here. ANNE gets up and goes to the TV and turns it on. An automobile commercial with romantic music.
JOE
We going to have more of that fashion shit?
ANNE
No. I'm looking for a soccer game, you asshole.
JOE
You want to dance?
ANNE
Yeah...
They do.
INT - BULGARI - NIGHT
KITTY runs into CHER.
KITTY
Oh! Cher! Hey. I'm Kitty Potter for FAD and this is Cher. Hey...
CHER
Hi.
KITTY
How are you doing?
CHER
Fine.
KITTY
Great. Are you enjoying this party. We're at the Bulgari party—
CHER
Yes, I am. I'm—yes.
KITTY
In Paris. At Paris. All right. Will you talk about it for us?
CHER
Well, yeah. I actually think the whole thing behind all of this Prêt-à-Porter and all of this thing is about women trying to be beautiful. None of us are going to look like Naomi Campbell, none of us are going to look like Christy Turlington, so in a way I think it's kinda sad...
KITTY
...and not many of us are going to look like you either so...
CHER
Well, yeah, I don't know. I mean, I'm a victim as well as a perpetrator of this. I think it's not about what you put on your body, it's about what you are on the inside.
INT - BULGARI PARTY - UPSTAIRS DINING ROOM
The ROMNEYS, JACK, KIKI, DANE, SLIM, and CLINT gather at a table.
ROMNEY
I'm starved. I'm starved.
KIKI
...yeah, we do. We worked for about a year now...
SLIM
At last, a table. A chair.
INT - BULGARI PARTY
KITTY bumps into ISABELLA.
KITTY
Madame de la Fontaine?
ISABELLA
Yes?
KITTY
May I introduce myself. I'm Kitty Potter.
ISABELLA
Oh, what a cute name.
KITTY
It's not real. It's just for TV.
ISABELLA
Mine is not real either.
KITTY

No, I know. It was your husband's name, right?
ISABELLA
Oh, not really. Excuse me.
KITTY
I love your jewels.
ISABELLA
Thank you.
Meanwhile, MAJOR talks to a fellow GUEST.
MAJOR
You understand English?
The GUEST walks away, blankly. SERGEI walks by in MAJOR's newly tailored clothes.
MAJOR
Hey, hey! I got a jacket just like that.
FIONA tries to interview REGINA KRUMM. CRAIG butts in.
CRAIG
'Scuse me. I'm sorry.
FIONA
I'm Fiona Ulrich. I'm from the <u>New York Times</u>. Hi.
REGINA
Hi.
FIONA
How are you?
REGINA
All right.
FIONA
I just wanted—how do you find this year's collection different from last year's?
REGINA
Uh—uh—uh, I don't know. I think I really have to see more. Some of what...
REGINA spots MILO showing a proof sheet to NINA.
NINA
Let me see this one of Regina...
REGINA
Um—would you excuse me. I have to go.
CRAIG
The drinks... there was just...
REGINA
Please, come!
She drags CRAIG away.
SERGEI has worked his way into a spot where he is behind ISABELLA and can talk to her without her seeing him. He speaks to her in Italian.
SERGEI
No, non ti voltare, non mi guardare, sono io Sergio, il tuo Sergio. (Don't turn around. Don't look at me. It's me, Sergio. Your Sergio.) Quanto tempo é passato, Sei sempre bellisima bella che mai. Ma quanti anni son passati, io capisco che tu sei convinta che ero morto et, quanti ani, quaranta, quarantadue? (How much time has gone by? You're more beautiful than ever. I thought you were convinced that I was dead. How many years? Forty, forty-two?) Non e possible. (How old were you?)
ISABELLA
Forse seidici anni (Maybe, sixteen years old.)
SERGEI
Diciotto mi pare. (Eighteen, I think.)
ISABELLA
Forse quindici. (I was fifteen.)
SERGEI
Già, era la mia sposa bambina. (Yes, you were my child bride.)
ISABELLA
Si eravamo proprio marito e moglie.
(Yes, we were really husband and wife, for sure.)
SERGEI
E come. (And then?)

167

ISABELLA
Eppure sei partito per Mosca quella stessa notte. (But you left for Moscow on our wedding night.)
SERGEI
Noi eravamo dei veri comunisti. (We were Communists. Remember?)
ISABELLA
Tu era comunista, io avevo appena solo quattordici anni. (You were a Communist, I was only fourteen years old.)
NINA is still looking at MILO's proof sheet. CY BIANCO has joined them.
NINA
Milo, you have to do a book. A book of tragedy. You have to.
MILO
No, that's so boring, you know.
SISSY WANAMAKER looks over in their direction and overhears the conversation.
NINA
Look at these tired old tits. I mean, quel tragic.
CY BIANCO
You gonna blackmail people or what?
MILO
You better watch out. I might get one of you.
BIANCO
I want a print of this one right here.
NINA
You have to do a book.
MILO
(putting the proofs away)
Aah, it passes the time anyway, you know.
SERGEI is still talking to ISABELLA.
SERGEI
Appena arrivato a Mosca, il giorno dopo Stalin mori. (The very day I arrived in Moscow, Stalin died.) I mutamenti, la confusione, le paure, lo spavento, (The changes, the confusion, fears and fright...) di qua, di la—non sapere dove andare; (I had no way to contact you.) Io non poteveo comunicare con te, come telefonarti, (I couldn't telegraph you? In the meantime, time went by.) come telegrafarti, nulla funzionavé. Intanto il tempo passava (My own life was in danger.) anche la mia vita é stata in pericolo (I had to change my identity, even my name.)io ho dovuto cambiare identita cambiare nome. (I gave myself a Russian name.) Mi sono spacciator per un Russo tu lo sai, io ero un sarto come mio padre (You know, I'm a tailor like my father.)ed ho comminaciato a fare dei vestiti per le signore di questi funzionare della nuova politica, ma... (I started to make clothes for the officials of the new government.) Poi un giorno su un giornale francese ho letto che ti eri resposata con Olivier de la Fontaine. (Then, one day, in a French newspaper, I read that you had married Olivier de la Fontaine.) E il mio cuore é spezzato. Lo ti amo ancora, ho lasciato... (My heart broke. I still love you, I left...)
At this point, a GUEST approaches ISABELLA.
GUEST
Isabella, I'm so sorry about the death of your husband.
ISABELLA
Thank you very much indeed.
MILO hands ALAIN, one of his entourage, his hotel room card key.
MILO
I want you to take them back to my hotel. There's the key. Okay?
ALAIN
Okay.
MILO
Bring the key back to me immediately.
ALAIN
No problem. I'll be back in a minute.
MILO gives ALAIN his hotel room key. We see that SISSY is overhearing this. SISSY pulls VIVIENE aside.

SISSY
Know that boy?
VIVIENE
Who? Oh! Alain! Yes. I know him.
SISSY
Good. Follow him. Get that key for me. Bring it back here before he gets back. Do you
understand?
VIVIENE
But how?
SISSY
I don't know how. That's what you're here for. Use your brain. Your breasts. Anything.
But get me that key.
VIVIENE
I don't think he likes girls.
SISSY
Well, then act like a boy.
SISSY pushes VIVIENE after ALAIN.
SERGEI is still talking to ISABELLA.
SERGEI
Non e stato un omicidio. Io lo so perche ero li. (De la Fontaine was not murdered. I
know, because I was there.)
ISABELLA
Tu eri la? (You were there?)
SERGEI
Si.
ISABELLA
E non hanno massato? (And you didn't kill him?) Che peccato. (What a shame.)
SERGEI
Dobbiamo vederci, domani io ti spieghero tutto. (We have to meet. Tomorrow, I'll explain
everything.) Vediamici domani in un posto dove... (At a place where we won't be
recognized.) Alle dieci, per esempio, sull Tour Eiffel. (At ten... at the Eiffel Tower.)
No meglio di no. Ecco nel giardino del Museo Rodin. Vicino alla statua del Pensatore alle
dieci. (No, too crowded. We'll meet at the Rodin Museum. At the statue of The Thinker. At
ten.)
ISABELLA
Ma io non mi alzo prima di mezzo giorno. (But I don't get up before noon.)
SERGEI
Alle dodici allora. (At twelve, then.)
ISABELLA
Alle dodici faccio l'aerobica. (At twelve, I have aerobics.)
SERGEI
Beh—alle quattro. (Well, at four.)
ISABELLA
Alle quattro. (Four is good.)
SERGEI
Ciao.
ISABELLA
Ciao.
BIANCO meets up with REGGIE.
BIANCO
I want to go back to the studio, do a little work down at the atelier. Some things I got
in my head.
REGGIE
Want me to come with you?
BIANCO
No, no. I'm—you just—you stay here.
REGGIE
All right.
INT - BULGARI PARTY - UPSTAIRS DINING ROOM
VIOLETTA excuses herself from the table.

169

BULGARI

VIOLETTA
I forgot.
ROMNEY
What?
VIOLETTA
Well, it's a surprise. Listen, don't ask me. It's a surprise, I can't tell you. Well, I'll meet you later at L'Arc. It's a surprise. Excuse me, everybody. Good-bye.
JACK gets up, kisses DANE on the cheek and starts to leave. KIKI grabs her cigarettes and gets up too.
JACK
Slim...
KIKI
I have a headache. I have to get going. Sorry. Bye sis.
DANE
Clint, do you mind helping me downstairs? I think I snapped my heel.
ROMNEY
Called nature.
CLINT
See ya, Slim.
SLIM is all alone at the table, abandoned.
At another table, a waiter approaches JEAN-PAUL GAULTIER with two bottles of wine.
WAITER
Blanc oú rouge? (White or red?)
GAULTIER
Je vais prendre du rosé s'il vous plaît. (I would like some rosé, please.)
WAITER
Voila!
GAULTIER
Bravo, bonne couleur! (Good color!)
INT - JOE & ANNE'S ROOM - NIGHT
JOE and ANNE going at it under the covers.
EXT - FOUNTAIN - NIGHT
FIONA and EVE are holding hands, and they walk past VIVIENE and ALAIN, who are making out. VIVIENE is trying to get MILO's room key.
At another part of the fountain, ROMNEY and BIANCO are sharing a joint.
And, nearby, VIOLETTA and REGGIE pass a whiskey flask back and forth.
As VIVIENE gets MILO's key out of ALAIN's pocket, he bites her breast, and, startled, she accidentally flings the key into the fountain. She jumps in to retrieve it.
INT - GRAND HOTEL - MILO'S SUITE - NIGHT
SERGEI enters MILO's room. He starts to go through MILO's closet. He picks out a suit. He hears a key in the door. He hides in the closet. SISSY comes into the room. She starts to rifle through MILO's negatives looking for the shots he took of her. She dumps negatives into a bag.
SISSY
Oh God! You evil son of a bitch.
She hears a noise, grabs the bag of negatives and starts to leave. Too late! The door opens. SISSY hides in the closet. MILO and NINA enter.
NINA
Oh God, I hate these stupid cards. Just give me a fucking key. I love keys. Now, do you have anymore of these photographs to show me?
MILO
C'mere you big gorilla.
NINA
Oh! You animal...
SISSY and SERGEI are now face to face in the closet. They are both startled but play it very cool.
NINA
Did you fart?
MILO
I never fart. And only when I drink champagne. You're a great shape of a woman.

NINA
Let me get my coat off.
MILO
You know that? I'm sick of all these models. They're like walkin' implants.
NINA
It's so hot.
MILO
C'mere. Sit down. Hey, do you want a drink?
NINA
Oh God, I'd love one. Lovely.
MILO
Do you like Irish whiskey?
NINA
I'd love it.
MILO
(hands her a bottle)
That's the good stuff.
NINA
Can I have a glass, please?
MILO
No, knock it back. You'll love it.
NINA
Oh, great.
MILO
C'mon, sit down. Relax.
NINA
Oh, you know, I just love Ireland. It's fantastic. It's so beautiful. We landed in
Shannon last year, and we drove around the ring of Kerry, which is unbelievably
beautiful. We stayed in a couple of hotels. They weren't bad—I think one was in the
Relais Château which is my bible. The people are fantastic. I don't think Irish people
are thick, I think you're lyrical and...
During this, MILO loads his spy camera. Then, he jumps over the sofa and pounces on NINA.
MILO
C'mere, you big animal.
NINA
You have no savoir faire, Milo.
MILO
C'mere. C'mere, I'll show you my boudoir.
NINA
Where are we going? Oh, your boudoir? I love—I love your use of the language.
MILO
Get that Gaultier stuff off ya.
NINA
I'll never get it over my Philip Treacy hat.
MILO
Philip Treacy? The Galway charlatan.
NINA
He's a genius.
MILO and NINA go into the bedroom and close the door. SISSY and SERGEI sneak out of the
closet. They quietly leave together.
INT - GRAND HOTEL - HALLWAY - NIGHT
SERGEI and SISSY come out of MILO's room: SERGEI with MILO's suit, SISSY with the photos.
SISSY
Bonsoir.
SERGEI
Bonsoir, Madame.
They take off in different directions.
INT - GRAND HOTEL - MILO'S SUITE - NIGHT
NINA storms out of the bedroom, covering herself with some of her clothes. The rest she
picks up from the living-room floor. She is furious. MILO is laughing.

NINA

Fucking photographs! Stop it! That's enough! No more! Stop taking fucking photographs, you animal. Jesus... I wondered what that clicking sound was. You must be gay if you want me in that position, anyway! You little shit. Don't take any more fucking photographs, you— Stop it! That's—I'll get the camera off you.

MILO

Good night.

NINA

Stop it! You Irish wanker! You Irish, you are thick, I take it back. You're fucking stupid! And you wouldn't know what to do with your fucking country if we gave it back to you. You bug-runner. Where's my bag? Jesus...

EXT - VIEW OF PARIS - SUNRISE

The sun rises over the city.

INT - JACK & DANE'S APARTMENT - DAY

JACK is just arriving home. The telephone is ringing.

JACK

Dane! The telephone is ringing!

He looks around the apartment. She's not there. He answers the phone.

JACK

Hello?

SIMONE (on phone)

What happened to my clothes? What are you doing with Milo O'Branagan? What's going on around here?

JACK

I can explain everything, mother.

SIMONE (on phone)

Oh, I doubt it.

DANE comes home.

JACK

(to DANE)

Where have you been all night? Huh?

SIMONE (on phone)

Hello?

JACK

I'll call you back.

He slams down the phone and follows DANE upstairs.

JACK

I want to know where you've been all night.

DANE

I spent the night with my sister. How 'bout you?

JACK is stymied.

INT - CORONER'S LAB - DAY

CORONER

Chaque mort paraît differente. Mais en fin de compte le resultat est toujours le même. La personne ne vit plus. (Each death seems so different. Yet, the results are always the same. The person no longer lives.) Un peu de croissant? (Some croissant?)

TANTPIS

Non merci.

CORONER

Quand on est mort, on est mort. (Dead is dead.)

TANTPIS

Quand saurons nous? (When will we know?)

CORONER

Oh, on sait. On sait déjà. Dès a present. (Oh, we know. We already know.)

TANTPIS

Qu'est ce qu'on sait? (What do we know?)

CORONER

On sait. On sait qu'il est mort. Indeniablement il est mort. (We know he is dead. That I am sure of.)

TANTPIS

Je sais qu'on sait qu'il est mort. Mais pourquoi est il mort? (I know we know he is dead. But why did he die?)
CORONER
Oh ? C'est une question difficile ça, pourquoi. Demain je pourrai vous dire comment. (Why? That's a difficult question. Why... Tomorrow, we will know how.)
TANTPIS
Demain?! (Tomorrow?!)
FORGET
Au moins une chose qu'on sait, c'est que les deux hommes avaient le même goût. (At least we know that the two men had the same taste.)
TANTPIS
Et comment savez vous cela? (And how do we know that?)
FORGET
Ils portaient la meme cravate. (Because they wore the same tie.)
INT - SONIA RYKIEL - RUNWAY - DAY
KIKI and DANE are among the MODELS.
INT - GRAND HOTEL - JOE & ANNE'S ROOM - SUNRISE
JOE lies in bed. ANNE is in the bathroom. The telephone rings and JOE knocks over last night's champagne glasses trying to answer it.
JOE
Hello?
CONCIERGE (on phone)
Mr. Flynn? This is the concierge. We have secured a room for you. I am sending the key right away.
JOE
Um—I don't want it.
ANNE sticks her head out the door, her mouth is full of toothpaste.
ANNE
Is it the laundry, or our bags or a room?
JOE
(covers phone, whispers)
My wife.
ANNE runs into the bathroom and locks the door.
CONCIERGE (on phone)
No, this is the concierge. The bellboy's bringing the new room key now.
JOE
No. I don't want it.
CONCIERGE (on phone)
We are sorry for the inconvenience.
JOE
I don't want it.
CONCIERGE (on phone)
I hope you enjoy your stay at the Grand Hotel.
JOE
No—écoute. C'mon, man... Hello?
INT - SONIA RYKIEL - BACKSTAGE - DAY
KITTY
Excuse me, you're on my cord? Thank you. My own cameraman. This is Kitty Potter... We're rolling? This is Kitty Potter live in Paris with the queen of knit: Sonia Rykiel. And—
SONIA RYKIEL
Thank you, thank you.
KITTY
It was a wonderful, sensual show. The collection was beautiful.
SONIA RYKIEL
Please, please. You speak too quick for me. Because my English is not too good. Can you translate for me?
KITTY
We need a translator here. I think we're having a little problem right here.
INT - GRAND HOTEL - HALLWAY - DAY
A BELLBOY knocks on JOE and ANNE's door. JOE, draped in sheets, opens the door.

BELLBOY
Ah, Mr. Flynn, c'est vôtre clef... (Mr. Flynn, this is the key...)
JOE
Sh-sh-sh. No, I don't want it.
BELLBOY
Mais c'est pas possible, regardez... (For your new room...)
JOE
What? Are you deaf? Are you deaf?
BELLBOY
Mais si, Mr. Flynn. Excusez moi. (But, Mr. Flynn, excuse me.)
JOE
I don't want it.
SERGEI, who has been walking down the hall, overhears this.
BELLBOY
Regardez c'est vôtre clef. (It's your key.)
JOE
I don't want it. Je suis pas vous. Understand? Good-bye. Au revoir. Good-bye. Au revoir. Au revoir.
JOE slams the door in the BELLBOY's face. SERGEI comes right up to him and says:
SERGEI
Oà étiez vous? Je suis la à vous attendre. Je suis, Mr. Flynn. Vous avez apporté ma clef. (Where have you been? I'm Mr. Flynn. Did you bring my key?)
The BELLBOY gives him the key and waits for a tip, which he doesn't get.
INT - GRAND HOTEL - MILO'S SUITE - DAY
MILO comes out of his bedroom in his robe.
MILO
Winnie! Where's my coffee. Do I have to do everything meself. Jesus Christ! What happened to the proofs? Winnie?! The proofs? What happened to the negatives!
INT - CY BIANCO'S SHOW - METRO STATION DEFILE - DAY
KITTY, SOPHIA, and FIONA are there. REGINA and MAJOR are in the audience. Standing in the back, wearing dark glasses and trying not to be noticed, is CORT ROMNEY.
KITTY
Where else would an underground designer go but underground? I'm standing in the crush of Cy Bianco's fans who've gathered here in an abandoned metro station to see what generation X wants to wear...
SOPHIE
Wait a minute...
KITTY
Wait a minute, what?
SOPHIE
There's Cort Romney.
KITTY
Oh! Wait a minute. Wait a minute. It's Cort Romney, who professes never to look at a fashion magazine and never visits anyone's atelier. Cort, to what do we owe this delightful pleasure?
CORT ROMNEY
I must've missed my stop. This obviously isn't Gare St. Lazare, is it?
INT - CY BIANCO'S SHOW - BACKSTAGE - DAY
CY BIANCO is busy dressing his MODELS. The show is about to start. INSPECTORS TANTPIS and FORGET arrive. DANE and KIKI are dressing next to one another.
KIKI
What's that supposed to mean?
DANE
I think you know exactly what it means.
KIKI
Hey, I'm not the one who's married, you know. You're the one who should be covering her ass. Not me.
DANE
At least I'm not fucking other people's husbands.
KIKI

So?
DANE
Somebody's fucking mine.
KIKI
I think you're being a bit neurotic. You don't know that anyway.
DANE
There's nothing neurotic about what I'm saying. I'm not being overly sensitive.
KIKI
Oh, how do you know? How do you know?
DANE
I can smell it on him. And it smells very close to home.
KITTY finishes her interview with CORT ROMNEY.
CORT ROMNEY
I have one more thing to say to the press in general and to you, Potty, in particular:
"How many g's are there in bugger off?".
KITTY
Well... what an artistic temperament!
INT - CY BIANCO SHOW - BACKSTAGE
REGGIE approaches CY BIANCO who is peeking at the audience.
REGGIE
Everything is all right?
BIANCO
Mm-hm.
REGGIE
Let me see.
BIANCO
Any spies out there? Vogue... Harper's Bazaar...
VIOLETTA enters. She is taking a seat, trying not to be noticed. NINA enters and sits
next to REGINA. NINA is still in a flap. SISSY enters and sits next to them. They are all
very cool toward each other. VIVIENE, CRAIG, and JEAN-PIERRE are there. MILO is there but
apart from the three editors.
SISSY
Well, I wonder who's going to sign Milo O'Branagan.
NINA
Well, Vogue is very happy that his contract is up, so I guess that leaves a clear track
for you two.
REGINA
Elle's not interested in has-beens.
SISSY
Really? I would have thought you'd be on your hands and knees to sign him? In fact, I
think you were.
REGINA
What did he tell you, Sissy?
SISSY
Nothing. Just something I saw.
REGINA
He showed you pictures of me?
SISSY
Let's just say I saw them. I haven't seen yours yet Nina, but I'm sure they're wonderful.
NINA
How do you know he took photographs of me?
SISSY
I was in the room.
NINA
What do you mean you were in the room.
SISSY
Well, I wasn't actually in the room, I was in the closet.
REGINA
He took photographs of all three of us?
SISSY

Yes, he did.
REGINA
...misery...
NINA
...psychopath...
SISSY
Yes, well not to worry, girls. Not to worry. I have the negatives of the Lammereaux boot shoot.
The lights dim, the show starts.
INT - SIMONE LO'S ATELIER - DAY
JACK and SIMONE are there. The TV is on. PILAR sits in the corner like a statue. She never moves through all the following.
SIMONE
You sold my company. You sold me to a Texan shoemaker?
JACK
Boots. A very rich bootmaker.
SIMONE
Without my permission? Without asking me? But who are you? You know, you're worse than your father?
JACK
Whoever that was.
SIMONE
You sell and buy everything. Even your own mother.
JACK
I did it for your own good, Mother.
SIMONE
My own good?
JACK
Yes.
SIMONE
Who decides? A philanderer? A traitor? A liar.
JACK
Merde! Qu'est-ce que tu veux? On n'a plus d'argent. (What do you want? We don't have any money!)
SIMONE takes a moment to think about all this.
SIMONE
And where are these people?
JACK
They're here.
SIMONE
Here?
JACK
They're outside. But it's a done thing, Mother. There's nothing you can do. I did it for you. You'll be rich now. You'll be rich.
SIMONE
Okay. Well, let them in. I want to meet my new boss.
JACK
You'll see. Things will turn out just great. You'll still be the designer. We won't have any more problems about money. You'll be just like Lagerfeld or Lacroix or Ferré.
JACK opens the door.
INT - CY BIANCO'S SHOW - METRO STATION DEFILE - DAY
KIKI and DANE, dressed like all the other MODELS, are on the runway at the same time. DANE bumps into KIKI. KIKI responds with an elbow in the ribs. Then, as they leave the runway to return backstage, they both go at it and it turns into a real cat fight.
EXT - RODIN GARDENS - DAY
SERGEI waits for ISABELLA at the foot of The Thinker statue. She approaches him and slaps him across the face. She spins and walks away. SERGEI recovers and chases after her.
SERGEI
Ma—ma perché? (But, but why?)
ISABELLA

Perché hai chiamato il mio secondo marito è non me? (Why did you contact my second husband and not me?)
SERGEI
Perché avevo paura che non mi volessi vedere. (Because I was afraid you wouldn't want to see me.)
ISABELLA
Perché avrei dovuto—eh?
Vuolevi ricattarlo farse? (You must have wanted to blackmail him?)
SERGEI
Ricattarlo farse? (Blackmail? Me?)
ISABELLA
Ma—per fortuna che é morto, l'hai ammazzato tu? (Well, thank goodness he's dead.) Lo spero, lo spero proprio. (I'm glad you killed him. I'm really glad.)
SERGEI
No, no, non l'ho ammazzato io, guarda io posso spiegarti tutto. (No, no, I didn't kill him. I can explain everything.)
ISABELLA
E spiega spiega. (Then explain, explain.)
SERGEI
Ecco dunque appena... (Well, it's a long story...)
INT - CY BIANCO'S SHOW - METRO STATION DEFILE - DAY
CY BIANCO takes the runway while the AUDIENCE cheers. He holds KIKI and DANE apart. NINA, REGINA, and SISSY run out as quickly as possible.
INT - CY BIANCO'S SHOW - BACKSTAGE - DAY
KITTY, SOPHIE, FIONA, MAJOR, CORT ROMNEY, VIOLETTA, VIVIENE, JEAN-PIERRE, CRAIG, INSPECTORS TANTPIS and FORGET have all gone backstage to congratulate BIANCO.
MAJOR
Cy? Major Hamilton. Marshall Field's. Chicago. Fashion director. I want to say what you're doing—what you're doing, is sensational. It's very adventurous. You're a real hero. Of course, it's not right for my place, you know. I mean, we're very traditional. You know, conservative. But maybe ten years down the line. Hold on a minute, I'm talking—
BIANCO
It's not right for everybody, right.
MAJOR
No, it isn't. The younger employees in my place all love your stuff...
BIANCO spots ROMNEY who motions for him to meet inside one of the metro cars. CY BIANCO goes to CORT ROMNEY.
Meanwhile, VIOLETTA and REGGIE look around for a private place to rendezvous. They see an empty metro car and head for it.
INT - METRO CAR
VIOLETTA and REGGIE sneak in and and start kissing. Unbeknownst to them, across the aisle, CORT ROMNEY and CY BIANCO are doing the same. Suddenly, everyone is aware of everyone else.
BIANCO
(To REGGIE)
Bitch!
REGGIE
You're the bitch.
ROMNEY
(To VIOLETTA)
Slut! How could you, you cunt!
VIOLETTA
No, you're the cunt.
REGGIE
What are you doing here?... What a liar.
ROMNEY
You're a tart... adulterer... mendacious...
VIOLETTA
Or is it Cy? Or are you both cunts?

KITTY pops her head in.
KITTY
Hi, Cy. Thought you were hiding from us.
The FAD TV CREW follows her into the metro car and quickly sets up for an interview. They
all become very friendly, covering the argument.
KITTY
Wonderful show, just wonderful. We loved it. Just loved it. Would you mind doing a little
thing with us? For FAD? Do you mind? Hi. Hi, everybody. Do you mind if I just get right
in here?
(re: her mike)
Can I have it? Okay. Can we roll? We're rolling? Okay, let's go. Hey everybody! Kitty
Potter coming at you from Cy Bianco's funkin' fashion show. Cy, that was super fun. Tell
us about the collection.
BIANCO
Uh—trying to do something like stocking tops, layers, you know. Old clothes. Taking old
clothes from like Tati, different places, and reshaping them really tight for the youth.
You know, not too expensive.
KITTY
Right.
REGGIE
Brilliant work.
ROMNEY
You are a pagan. You are to the 90s what lava lamps were to the 70s.
KITTY
Oh, I loved it. We loved it.
REGGIE
I'm proud of you.
ROMNEY
It's perfect. It says go-go-go. It's plastic, it's rap, it's fabulous, it's Cy.
INT - GRAND HOTEL - MILO'S SUITE - NIGHT
SLIM walks in with MILO.
SLIM
This circus is driving me crazy.
WINNIE
Hi, Miss Chrysler.
SLIM
It's more like a soccer match, you know, than it is a fashion show. And my feet are
killing me. I can not find any shoes to wear in this town...
MILO
Well, at least they match...
SLIM
What do you mean they match? Of course, they match. They always match. What are you
talking about?
MILO
Do you want some tea or coffee?
SLIM
No, I need a drink. A stiff drink. Uh—Irish whisky.
MILO
Sure. Give her some Irish whiskey, will ya?
WINNIE
Oh—well there's none left. You finished it.
MILO
Well order up some more, will ya?.
SLIM
Oh! Lookie, lookie. This is what I've been waiting for...
MILO
No, that's the Rykiel shoot.
SLIM
Oh... Well, where are the proofs?
MILO

Oh, well, there's a problem with the proofs.
SLIM
Oh, I was afraid of that. I mean, the boot idea didn't work?
MILO
No, the boots worked fine. It's just that there's a problem with the negatives.
The doorbell rings.
WINNIE
I'll get that. Don't worry.
SLIM
Milo... are you trying to tell me the lab fucked up?
MILO
No, I'm not trying to tell you the lab fucked up. But there is a fuckup with the negatives.
SLIM
Well, what am I going to tell Clint? I mean, you know, he seems very quiet on the outside, but he can be a real monster.
SISSY, NINA, and REGINA enter. All three are wearing sunglasses.
SLIM
Well... what do we have here? A publishers' convention?
The three editors sit on the sofa.
MILO
Looks like a scene from Macbeth.
SISSY
Negotiations.
SLIM
What she say?
MILO
She said, "Negotiations."
EXT - HOTEL SPLENDID - NIGHT
LOUISE is on her balcony overlooking the Arc de Triomphe. She calls to MAJOR.
LOUISE
Oh, this is so beautiful. Come outside. Come here and look at this view. It is so beautiful.
MAJOR
You're the only view I want to see...
They kiss.
LOUISE
Oh, honey. Come inside. I want to show you some of the things I bought today. C'mere.
LOUISE takes MAJOR inside. Next door is FIONA's room. FIONA is trying on and discarding one outfit after another. EVE is on TV being interviewed.
EVE
Oui... j'aime pas les piercings. Je trouve pas ça esthetic. (I don't like piercings. I don't find it esthetic.)
REPORTER
Vous en avez eu marre d'etre chauve? (Were you tired of being merely bald?)
EVE
Non, pas du tout, non, non. C'est juste c'est une surprise. (No, not at all. No, no, it was just a surprise.)
Meanwhile, LOUISE shows MAJOR her purchases.
LOUISE
This is the Sonia Rykiel I was talking to you about. What a beautiful color.
MAJOR
It's gorgeous. I love the color.
LOUISE
This is beautiful.
MAJOR
Material's beautiful.
LOUISE
It's kind of a Chinese thing with the little frogs on the side.
MAJOR

Aha! That's nice.
LOUISE
Isn't that a very beautiful thing...
MAJOR
It's nice and long though, too.
LOUISE
Now, wait. Oh—This is the pièce de résistance. You can't believe... It's an opera coat!
MAJOR
Wow! Whoa!
LOUISE
This is beautiful, isn't it.
MAJOR
Victorian. Elizabethan.
LOUISE
I know, it's lovely. It's lovely.
Now, this is, of course, the best.
MAJOR
Oh, stop...
LOUISE
It's a Chanel suit!
FIONA is still dressing in the other room. EVE is on TV.
EVE
Non, justement c'est pas étrange c'est, ça prouve qu'y a des gens qui, qui, pensent pas seulement. (No, It's not strange. It shows that there are people who don't just think...) Je veux dire, on va toutes viellir puis on va toutes être laide dans une couple d'années, donc... (I mean, we're all gonna grow old. We're all gonna be ugly in a couple of years, anyway...)
INT - JOE & ANNE'S ROOM
ANNE is sneaking clean underwear out of her suitcase hidden in the closet. JOE discovers this.
ANNE
Ooops.
JOE
When did that come?
ANNE
Well, this afternoon. This morning.
JOE
Where was I?
ANNE
Sleeping.
There's a knock at the door. JOE answers.
JOE
Ah, my bagage.
A PORTER enters with JOE's lost luggage and a bottle of champagne.
PORTER #1
On a retrouvé vos bagages, monsieur Flynn. (We found your luggage, Mr. Flynn.) En fait ils n'étaient pas aux bagages perdus, ils étaient aux bagages trouvés. (It was not with lost luggage, it was with found luggage.) Avec les compliments de l'hotel. (With compliments of the hotel.) Bonsoir.
ANNE
Merci.
JOE
Merci, monsieur.
EXT - HOTEL SPLENDID - NIGHT
FIONA hails a cab.
INT - SIMONE LO'S SHOW - REHEARSAL
KITTY and SOPHIE are backstage.
KITTY
Hey there, again. This is Kitty Potter, giving you a glimpse of fashion-in-the-making. We're behind the scenes at Simone Lo as she rehearses her show. And from what we can tell

PRET-A-PORTER

here, all those models will be wearing, none other than, cowboy boots! Let's look around and see what else we can find.

As KITTY reports, we see SLIM and PILAR on the runway, choreographing the MODELS. Backstage, several MODELS are trying on CLINT's cowboy boots. KIKI and DANE, who are working the show, are apparently best of friends now. JACK tries to talk to DANE but both girls giggle when he comes around and ignore him.

JACK
Dane. We have to talk.

DANE
(To KIKI)
Did you hear something?

KIKI
No, Maybe just a rat.

DANE
Are there rats here?

JACK
Dane—

KIKI
But they're harmless, darling...

DANE
Harmless, yes. But so dégueulasse.

KIKI
And they just keep nibbling away.

DANE
I know.

JACK
Hello Eve.

INT - CROSS-DRESSER'S RESTAURANT - NIGHT
FIONA interviews some of the cross-dressers.

FIONA
What would you say is the difference between a cross-dresser and a transvestite?

CROSS-DRESSER
Well, actually, cross-dresser is just another way of saying transvestite, which is the same thing but coming from the Latin root.

FIONA
How do you choose what you're going to wear?

CROSS-DRESSER
Ah! This is the big problem. This is the big problem. Yeah, because I have many things, and it is very difficult to know what to wear from one situation to the other.

FIONA
You dress very elegantly. Is that something you look for when you choose your clothing?

CROSS-DRESSER
Yes, of course, and to be able to laugh about yourself. And take it easy. We are here to have a good time.

INT - SIMONE LO'S SHOW - REHEARSAL
KITTY
You guys go and look for some—uh—just look for some color. I don't know, something. I've got something in my shoe that's killing me.

SLIM passes by KITTY to give a pair of mismatched boots to a MODEL.

SLIM
Hi, honey. Put these on. They'll look great with that outfit.

MODEL
Okay, thanks. What, is she kidding?

KITTY
Is she color-blind? Those boots don't even match.

SOPHIE
Well, everybody knows that.

KITTY
Knows what?

SOPHIE

That she's color-blind.
KITTY
Well, I didn't.
SOPHIE
'Cause I didn't write it on your cards.
INT - GRAND HOTEL - NIGHT
ISABELLA
Bella stanza meravigliosa, non somiglia per niente a quella che avevano a Napoli, vediano un po questo letto? (Beautiful room. Marvelous. Doesn't look at all like the one we had in Naples. Let's try out the bed.)
ISABELLA sits on the bed.
ISABELLA
Senti ti ricordi la stanza che noi aviamo a Napoli? Piccola, piccola, cosi.(Do you remember the room we had in Naples? It was tiny, tiny like this.)
SERGEI
A Napoli, Isabella, mia avessi vista quella che avevo a Mosca, piccola cosi. (You should have seen the one I had in Moscow.)
ISABELLA
Ma va. E come for cheri a lavorare? (And how did you manage?)
SERGEI
Eh quattro metri quadrati, a Mosca le case non si trovano, io avevo atelier e letto tutto insieme. (Houses are hard to find. I had my workshop and bed all in one room.) Taglia e cuci, taglia e cuci tutto sopra il letto. (Cut and sew, cut and sew. Everything on the bed.) State anni bruti sei. (Those were terrible times, you know.)
ISABELLA
Poverino, e come facevi a lavorare? (Poor thing. And on your own without me.) Che c'e? (What's wrong?)
SERGEI
Che hanno bussato? (Did somebody knock?)
ISABELLA
No, no sei tropo agitato, calmati. (No, no. Relax. Calm down.)
SERGEI
Eh-beh, son tre notti che non dormo. (Well, I haven't slept for three nights.)
ISABELLA
Perché? (Why?)
SERGEI
E perché cerco te. (I was looking for you.)
ISABELLA
Ma figurati, che ci creda. (Were you really?)
SERGEI
Una sigarreta? (Cigarette?)
ISABELLA
No io non ho mai fumato. (No. I don't smoke.)
SERGEI
Lo invece se non fumo... Mi calma la sigaretta. (You don't smoke... Cigarettes calm me down.)
ISABELLA
Ah si?
SERGEI
Sono Russe. (They're Russian.)
ISABELLA
Je ne fume pas. I don't smoke.
SERGEI
Don't smoke—Inglese. Invece a Mosca dicono "spasiba niet papirofski." (In Moscow they say: "Spasiba niet papirofski.")
ISABELLA
Papiros.
SERGEI
Gia e vero, tu non fumavi. (It's true. You didn't smoke.)
ISABELLA

Ma no, io ero una bambina di quattordici anni come facevo a fumare? (Oh no, I was a baby.
I was only fourteen years old. How could I smoke?)
SERGEI
Quattordici anni. (Fourteen.)
ISABELLA
Quattordici anni. (Fourteen.)
SERGEI
Mamma mia, ma quanti anni sono Isabella? (My darling, how many years has it been?)
SERGEI attempts to kiss ISABELLA. She pushes him away.
ISABELLA
No ti prego. No, Sergio... (No, please. No, Sergio...)
INT - CROSS-DRESSER'S RESTAURANT - NIGHT
LOUISE arrives with MAJOR, who is wearing a wig and the Chanel suit.
MAJOR/MAY ROSE
Look at it... It's beautiful.
LOUISE
May Rose, you are beautiful. You look beautiful tonight. You do.
MAJOR/MAY ROSE
That's because you went shopping for me, darling. No one shops like my Louise.
LOUISE
Yes.
MAJOR/MAY ROSE
It's beautiful.
LOUISE
Very nice. Oooh.
MAJOR/MAY ROSE
What do you think?
LOUISE
Shall we join someone over there or...
MAJOR/MAY ROSE
I'd rather be alone tonight.
LOUISE
You want to be alone, okay.
INT - GRAND HOTEL - HOTEL ROOM - NIGHT
ISABELLA and SERGEI are wearing bathrobes. She doesn't have the intention of leaping
straight into bed.
ISABELLA
No, no, no, ti prego Sergio, ti prego. (No, no, no Sergio. Please don't.) Vai sal betto.
Non ti vicordi prui, non ti vicordi prui. (Get on the bed. Don't you remember? Have you
forgotten?) Vai li, vai li... (Go over there, over there...)
ISABELLA starts to strip. SERGEI howls, thrilled. Then, he falls asleep and snores.
INT - SIMONE LO'S SHOW - REHEARSAL - NIGHT
Out front, SIMONE and PILAR are working with lights, music, and MODELS to perfect the
show for the next morning. A few FRIENDS (REAL PEOPLE) sit in the AUDIENCE. ALBERTINE
arrives, waves to SIMONE. SIMONE hands PILAR the microphone and walks backstage to confer
with ALBERTINE.
INT - CROSS-DRESSERS' RESTAURANT
LOUISE
You know who you look like?
MAJOR/MAY ROSE
Who?
LOUISE
It just hit me. Just a little tiny bit. Barbara Streisand. In the eyes.
MAJOR/MAY ROSE
You really think so?
LOUISE
A little bit.
FIONA begins snapping photographs of the cross-dressers. MAJOR spots her.
MAJOR
Hey, you. You with the camera. I know you. I know who you are. Gimme that camera!

185

LOUISE
Quiet!
MAJOR/MAY ROSE
(to LOUISE)
I'll take care of this. Be right back.
(to FIONA)
Come back with that camera!
FIONA runs out of the restaurant.
LOUISE
Stop... stop.
MAJOR/MAY ROSE
Stop her! Come back with that camera! Stop her! She's got my camera! Stop that girl! Stop her! She stole my camera!
LOUISE
Oh, dear.
MAJOR/MAY ROSE
Stop that girl!
EXT - CROSS-DRESSERS' RESTAURANT - NIGHT
MAJOR chases FIONA down the street.
MAJOR/MAY ROSE
Come back here!
FIONA
Please, please sir. C'mon...
LOUISE bangs on the restaurant window.
LOUISE
May Rose. May Rose. It's me up here. Don't run like that.
MAJOR/MAY ROSE
Gimme that camera, you bitch.
FIONA
I'm not going to do anything with them...
MAJOR/MAY ROSE
Stop that girl! She stole my camera! Come back here!
INT - GRAND HOTEL - HOTEL ROOM #2 - NIGHT
SERGEI snores. ISABELLA finishes getting dressed. She scribbles a note on the dresser. She leaves quietly. CAMERA MOVES in on a CLOSE SHOT of the note. It reads: (in Italian) "Two husbands, two corpses."
INT - STAIRWAY - PREFECTURE DE POLICE - DAY
INSPECTOR TANTPIS is with FORGET. He is waiting for the reporters in order to announce the Olivier de la Fontaine case closed.
TANTPIS
Alors aujourd'hui, les circonstances de la mort de Monsieur Olivier de la Fontaine apparaissent (I would like to say that the shocking circumstances of Olivier de la Fontaine's death) moins bizarres et choquantes qu'elles ne sont apparues auparavant (are not so shocking). Monsieur Olivier de la Fontaine est mort de son incapacité a deglutir un corps étranger bloquant son oesophage (Mr. de la Fontaine has died from a blockage of the esophagus), corps étranger s'avérant être un morceau de gras de jambon (confirmed to be a morsel of ham fat). L'obstruction empêchant toute respiration naturelle a entraine (the obstruction had stopped his breathing) la suffocation et finalement la mort (to the point of suffocation and death).
INT - GRAND HOTEL - JOE & ANNE'S ROOM - DAY
JOE watches INSPECTOR TANTPIS's report on SKY TV.
ANNE comes out of the bathroom. She is dressed to the teeth in a great outfit. She spins around, showing off for JOE. JOE is in his original wardrobe (THE SUIT SERGEI ALTERED). It doesn't fit him. The pants are at least five inches too short. The jacket doesn't fit.
JOE
This guy wasn't even murdered. He choked on a sandwich. What a waste of time.
ANNE
A complete waste of time.
JOE
So, what do you think? I feel like I've grown since I've met you. So, what would you

186

write about this charming ensemble in your column, Anne?
ANNE
I'd say it's um... very Prêt-à-Porter.
JOE
You look great.
ANNE
So.
JOE
So.
ANNE
I really had a great time.
JOE
Me too. If uh—
ANNE
I think your—um... It was very nice to meet you, Mr. Joe Flynn.
JOE
It was very nice meeting you Anne... uh... Nixon.
ANNE
Eisenhower.
ANNE leaves the room.
INT - SIMONE LO'S SHOW - DEFILE - DAY
People are filing in, including SLIM, CLINT, SISSY, NINA, REGINA, FIONA, VIVIENE, CRAIG, JEAN-PIERRE, MILO, KITTY, and SOPHIE. The stage dims, and we hear the voice of Simone Lo in the loudspeakers:
SIMONE
This is Simone Lo. The collection you are about to see represents two decades of an emerging vision. For me, it's the closing of a circle... and the beginning of something new... something new... new... new...
The music starts. The lights come on, and the MODELS come out. They are stark naked. One after another they march down the runway. The audience is stunned. Then they laugh. Then they applaud. ALBERTINE (eight months pregnant) appears at the end as a naked bride, with veil and bouquet. It is all quite beautiful. SLIM, CLINT, and JACK are appalled. KITTY and SOPHIE rush from their seats and find their crew.
KITTY
We rolling?
FAD CAMERAMAN
Yes.
KITTY
This is Kitty Potter live from Paris at Simone Lo's défilé. Well, what can I say? Simone Lo has shown us everything. I mean, I don't know how much of this is going to be on TV or anything but... It's so new, I mean, you know, it's so... it's so old. I mean, she shows it like it really is. It's so old it's true. It's so true, it's new. It's the oldest new look. It's the newest old look. It's—it's... Simone Lo has created a New-New Look for every man, woman and child, and they can all can afford it. It's called the Bare Look. So, hooray for Simone Lo!
KITTY breaks here and stops the camera.
KITTY
What the hell am I talking about? For Chrissakes, what is going on here, really? What's going on here on this planet? This is fuckin' fruitcake time. I mean, is that fashion? Is it? I mean is there a message up there? I mean, you got a lot of naked people wandering around here... I mean, I have been forever trying to figure out what this bullshit is about... And you know what? You know what? I have had it. I have had it! Good-bye. Au revoir. Sophie! You've got yourself a career.
She hands Sophie the mike and walks away.
SOPHIE
This is Sophie Choiset for FAD-TV. In May 1968, the great couturier Balenciaga closed his atelier forever because, he said, "There is no one left to dress." It appears Simone Lo believes the same. She has just shown us a celebration of "fashion" in the profoundest sense of the word. She has made a statement here today that will be felt for decades to come... she has made a choice that will influence all designers everywhere... and most of

D3035
MIRAMAX FILMS

PRET-A -PORTER
PHOTO: E. GEORGES

all, she has spoken to women the world over, telling them not what to wear, but how to think... about what they want and need from fashion.
The show is over. The AUDIENCE claps enthusiastically. At the end of the runway, a curtain with the "Lo" logo rises revealing SIMONE, her STAFF and the MODELS. Everyone is naked including SIMONE and PILAR.
EXT. - CEMETERY ROAD IN PARIS - DAY
A somber but stylish funeral procession passes along the road. It's the funeral of OLIVIER DE LA FONTAINE. Everyone is dressed in black except for ISABELLA who wears bright colors. She also wears an extravagant and chic hat.
EXT - CEMETERY AREA -DAY
The PROCESSION passes. CAMERA moves in to see ISABELLA pass by SERGEI who's asleep on a bench. SERGEI, unshaven and groggy, is awakened by the procession.
EXT - PARK - GRASSY PARK AREA - DAY
Several naked BABIES are playing in the grass. CAMERA PULLS AWAY to reveal that it is a MILO O'BRANAGAN photo shoot. His ENTOURAGE is with him.
MILO
Okay, go on, put the diapers on the kids, will you?
Two assistants put diapers on two of the babies. The assistants carry the babies over to a large billboard. It's an advertisement for Trussarda showing a naked man and woman and the slogan, GET REAL.
MILO
Okay, let's go.
Meanwhile, the last of OLIVIER'S FUNERAL PROCESSION passes by SERGEI's bench. SERGEI gets up and follows the MOURNERS into the cemetery.

theend

Acknowledgments

Enormous thanks to Robert Altman for being Robert
Altman; to Scott Bushnell and Jim McLindon for their
invaluable support and help; to Harvey and Bob
Weinstein for their constant trust and enthusiasm; to
Fabien Baron for his brilliant vision, and Malin
Ericson for her assisting so ably; to Brian D. Leitch
for writing; to Woody Hochswender for editing; to
Scott Greenstein for fighting all the battles; and to
Delilah Bosanquet for her persistence.

Special acknowledgments go to the designers, all the
stars, photographers, and many others who contributed
to this book. In particular, to Barbara Shulgasser,
Hippolyte Romain, Helmut Newton-Sygma, Catherine
Leterrier, Philip Treacy, Etienne Georges, Rul
Benegas, Stephane Cardinale, Joakim von Ditmar,
Harris from Paris, Didier Robcis, Hugues Roussas,
Yannis Vlamos, Nino and Chantal Cerruti, Gianfranco
Ferré, Vivienne Westwood, Sonia Rykiel, Thierry
Mugler, Lamine Kayote, Tracey Ullman, Richard E.
Grant, Kim Basinger, Julia Roberts, Rossy de Palma,
Ute Lemper, Sophia Loren, Lauren Bacall, Stephen Rea,
Rupert Everett, and Georgianna Robertson.

And finally, thanks go to Carlo Ponti; Lisa Atkin;
Hiro Clark; Donna Daniels and Ivana Lowell; Craig
Nelson, Lauren Marino, and the rest of Hyperion;
Denise Breton; Jane Cattani; Eliane Laffont and Randi
Coran; Michael Foster; Elaine Goldsmith and Nancy
Seltzer; Davide Manfredi; Harriet Wilson; Condé Nast
Publications, Ltd.; and The Observer.

—Francesca Gonshaw, Editorial Director

With fondness and very special thanks to Robert
Altman. Special thanks to Marian Lacombe, Catherine
Pouligny, and Pascal Mourier of M6 for all of their
kind assistance. Also, Woody Hochswender, Susan
Walker, Andrew Marcus, Catherine Leterrier, Francesca
Gonshaw, Delilah Bosanquet, Scott Bushnell, Jim
McLindon, and Geraldine Peroni.

—Brian D. Leitch

First published in Great Britain in 1995 by
Boxtree Limited, Broadwall House, 21 Broadwall, London SE1 9PL

First published in the United States by
Hyperion, 114 Fifth Avenue, New York, NY 10011

ISBN 0-7522-0617-6

First Edition

1 3 5 7 9 10 8 6 4 2

A CIP catalogue entry for this book is available from the British Library.